Katie Wheeler 2/26

P9-DDC-620

HIGH SCHOOL
sports leader

Pass it on!

Use this space to write a note of encouragement,
advice, or inspiration to the recipient of this book.

Online Resources!

HIGH SCHOOL **sportsleader.com** In addition to the *High School Sports Leader* book, visit www.highschool sportsleader.com for additional articles, videos, and leadership tools.

A seasonal newsletter filled with new content is available to athletes, coaches, and athletic directors. Sign up today to receive a free article, "Turning down the volume on complaining teammates." The article is packed with ideas and strategies to create and maintain a positive atmosphere in your sport.

Package Pricing is Available!

Schools, conferences, and organizations interested in special quantity pricing for the *High School Sports Leader* book should visit www.highschoolsports leader.com.

Live Workshops!

To schedule a live leadership workshop with Craig Hillier visit www.craighillier.com.

About the Author

Craig Hillier has spoken in front of more than 2 million teenagers since his career started in 1990. His high-energy programs and contagious enthusiasm captivate audiences throughout the United States. In addition to leadership keynotes and school assemblies, Craig focuses his efforts on student leadership training. His programs are upbeat, fun, and educational. Craig recently received the Distinguished Alumni Award presented by the Minnesota State High School Athletic Administrators.

Craig is the author of *Playing Beyond the Scoreboard* and *How to Step Up as a Teen Leader*. He lives in Lakeville, Minnesota. He and his wife Kelly are blessed with two adult children, DJ and Abigayle.

Craig believes he was put on this earth to work with teenagers!

Coaching Team Leaders and Captains to a Season of Significance

A Winning Edge Seminars Publication
16759 Draft Horse Court
Lakeville MN 55044

612.749.9700
email: craig@craighillier.com
websites: www.highschoolsportsleader.com
        www.craighillier.com

ISBN: 978-0-965782-8-3
Copyright © 2016

All rights reserved. No part of this book may be used or reproduced in any manner whatsoever without written permission, except in the case of quotations.

Clip art purchased from by Shutterstock.
Cover photo by Peter Wong.

Dedication

Special thanks to my wife Kelly who patiently stuck with me on this journey as a speaker and author. Kelly is my brainstorm partner, editor, and most importantly my wife and life partner. Thanks to my two kids, Abigayle and DJ, who make life better through your laughter and wise comments.

Acknowledgments

I would like to thank my incredible editor Leslie Wilhelm Hatch. She tirelessly worked through my random thought process and helped me create the book I set out to write.

Finally, I'd like to thank my incredible clients throughout the United States who have supported my programs and partnered with me to motivate leaders to create a season of significance. It's been my joy to work with you over my career.

Contents

The GREAT*Full* CAUSE

Supporting **GREAT** Causes to Lead a *Full* Life.

Committing our talents and resources to **great** causes creates a *full* life. **Greatfull** people understand their lives improve when they develop a spirit of giving.

Today's world is overflowing with opportunities to help others and support worthwhile causes, both near and far. Whether it's a fundraiser for someone enduring a difficult situation or an educational scholarship to assist a student who has demonstrated outstanding leadership, it's important to contribute more than we consume. As the saying goes, with great privilege comes great responsibility.

My vision and goal with this book is to have a large impact on the audience that reads it *and* impact others who have not read it. Helping others not only makes me feel good, but it adds an increased sense of purpose and meaning to this book.

A percentage of the sale from each book purchased will be deposited into my **Greatfull** *Cause* account. When a worthy opportunity arises to financially help an individual or group, a check will be issued from this account.

Thank you! I am incredibly excited about the notion that a community of readers can support a variety of great causes.

This book is about creating both an athletic season of significance and a life of significance.

Let's face it. Only a handful of individuals or teams will ever win a state championship or play at the college level; far fewer will become professional athletes. While I hope you experience one of these levels of athleticism, I'm more interested in sharing ideas and strategies that will become a launching pad for the rest of your life.

High school sports provide countless life lessons, many of which are incredibly positive. And yet, candidly speaking, some of the lessons may be quite difficult to handle. Either way, the lessons can be pivotal in shaping the rest of your life.

Of course, athletics are not for everyone. Participating in a different extracurricular activity or club, however, can teach you the exact same principles. When you view a high school activity as an opportunity to learn and grow, every experience and lesson will be useful as you prepare for a life of significance!

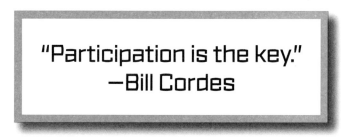

"Participation is the key."
—Bill Cordes

Leadership is a process—not an event.

Maybe a parent, a coach, or an athletic director presented this book to you. Whoever handed it to you hopes that the content will provide the *insight* and *inspiration* to lead your team to a new level.

You should understand, however, that you don't read one book, attend one seminar, or have one leadership experience and suddenly know all the ins and outs of leadership. Although no single resource will provide all the answers for team

leaders and captains, the conversations, workshop evaluations, and emails I receive from students indicate the ideas presented in this book can be game-changers. Of course, you will have to dig into it and implement the strategies to see the results. My promise is this: If you are even semi-serious about becoming a better leader, this book is for you.

All Sports Are Important

Writing a book universal to all sports is impossible. There are many different dynamics in high school sports. Some sports feature an individual component and a team component. Other sports are totally team driven, and there are no post-season individual tournaments. Despite these differences, it's vital to understand this: **All sports are important!**

As you work through this material, please be wise enough to read the concepts or stories and then adapt them to your sport as applicable. Some of the ideas or stories will transfer easily to your sport, whereas other concepts will not be as easy to adapt. Your goal is to implement the material that fits, while recognizing some content will not pertain to you or your sport.

A defining moment

It's a day I'll remember forever. I was a junior walking down the high school hallway. We had just wrapped up a rather dismal basketball season and had our year-end team meeting the previous week. The head coach stopped me in the hallway and simply said, "Craig. Good news. You've been selected co-captain for next year. All the coaches and your teammates are expecting big things from you. Congratulations! I'll see you later."

Why write this book?

Like most athletes who hear great news like this, I started to imagine being the first player to run on the court for warm-ups when the band started to play our fight song, "Here Come the Cardinals." It would be fun meeting with the officials before the game. I could hear our announcer saying, "At forward... team captain... number 33... Craig Hillier." It was going to be awesome!!!

However, the excitement was replaced quickly with anxiety. Questions started blazing through my head. What do I do now? Am I capable of filling this role? I'm not the best player on the team, how will that work? Will the other guys listen to me? How are we going to be better next year? Should I start planning captain's practices now? The questions didn't seem to end.

Unfortunately, there were no manuals, no online resources to access, no live workshops to attend that would prepare me to lead the team. Basically, I was on my own and was given the job without any instructions or guidelines. My captain-training program was a combination of watching how previous team captains operated and a single phrase from my coach, "Come on, be a leader!" Maybe you have heard this comment before and asked yourself, "What does that even mean?"

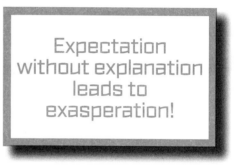

Expectation without explanation leads to exasperation!

My experience as a team captain that year was mostly trial and error. There were some great moments when the team bonded, and we upset teams with more talent than we had. There were also moments of frustration where team chemistry started to fall apart, and players started to turn on each other. There were many situations I wasn't expecting and didn't know how to handle. I often wondered if I was doing a good job. I found myself wishing for a resource to help me take the *guesswork* out of being a high school leader.

Realizing a need

The experience of being a **team leader** for a football team and a **team captain** for the basketball team became the motivation behind writing my second book, *Playing Beyond the Scoreboard—A Team Captain's Guide to a Season of Significance.* I wrote it in 2002. The results have been amazing and humbling. More than 55,000 of the original books are in print. It's encouraging to have conversations with students who have read the book and applied the concepts in their sport and in their lives.

I'm not trying to *impress* you as a reader. Rather, I'd like to *express* my appreciation to all the athletic directors,

coaches, and especially athletes who have implemented the book's ideas and strategies and committed themselves to developing their leadership abilities.

Since 2002, I have continued to learn and teach the keys to effective leadership to high school students. It has been exciting to conduct live workshops and have students suggest additional topics they would like to discuss. The combination of learning, growing, parenting, and listening to my audiences of athletic leaders motivated me to write a new book, *High School Sports Leader—Coaching Team Leaders and Captains to a Season of Significance.* It was written to harvest the shared wisdom I've gained since *Playing Beyond the Scoreboard* was written.

Before we continue, it's important to grasp the concept on the next page.

"There are some
team leaders
who are not team
captains.

There are some
team captains
who are not
team leaders!"

—Craig Hillier

As I've previously stated, I was a *team leader* for football and a *team captain* for basketball. Because our class had a lot of leaders, our football coach named new captains each week. This approach worked well because it would have been very difficult for the team or the coaching staff to narrow down the field to just a few team captains for the entire season. Rotating team leaders allowed several young men to experience a leadership role.

Basketball was different. Our team required a stronger structure; therefore, we had two captains who represented the team for the entire season. There were also more formal responsibilities for the basketball program including planning off-season practice and planning team bonding events and strategy meetings with the coaching staff. In football, due to the rotating captain approach, the coaches took on some of the tasks a team captain would normally undertake.

It's important to remember that every sports program is a little different in how it operates. Coaches adopt a variety of beliefs when it comes to team leadership.

What might work with one team during a certain year won't work next year. And what works with one sport may not work with a different sport. There is not a perfect system.

Athletic directors and coaches often ask me, "What's the best way to name captains?" The answer is simple. It depends on the team and its needs!

Whether you are an athlete who is interested in leadership, already an influential team leader, or an elected team captain, **High School Sports Leader** will guide you through the ins and outs of making a positive difference. This positive difference will most definitely bring significance to your sports season, but can also bring significance to your life and the life of your teammates.

The content of this book is similar to a vast buffet served at a restaurant. The buffet will feature foods you:

- ▶ Love
- ▶ Like but don't love
- ▶ Don't like based on previous experience
- ▶ Have never tried but inspire your curiosity
- ▶ Have never heard of or seen

You will have the same reactions to the ideas and concepts in this book. For the book to work for you, be willing to read and *diges*t the material. Be willing to try some of the strategies that may be new to you and see if you can expand your leadership *palate.*

Finally, be aware that some of the content may not be useful now, but may be useful in the future. You may read a chapter that doesn't seem relevant today, but a situation may present itself tomorrow. You'll want to return to the book for further study. In addition, the book will have a different meaning each time you read it. Some students have attended my live workshop first as a sophomore, and they returned as a senior. Although the workshops may have been similar, two years of leadership experience and maturity between the workshops changes the way they apply the information.

"Consume the best and don't worry about the rest," is a great way to get the most out of this book. Similar to the buffet analogy, most people will revisit it to fill up and refuel.

Overview of the book

I have invested a tremendous amount of time in the design and structure of this book. For teams that do not have official team captains, the team leader section will be the most useful. If a team identifies official captains, both team leaders **and** team captains can benefit from the material.

Part 1: Team Leader's Section

This section provides the foundation for leadership.

This section will be most beneficial to:

- ▶ Team leaders who are not team captains

- ▶ Students who may be elected/selected as future team captains

- ▶ Athletes who have already been named team captains

- ▶ Any athlete that wants to develop his or her leadership abilities

Part 2: Team Captain's Section

Many team captains have additional responsibilities that team leaders may not be asked to perform. This section provides addition information that will be essential for a season of significance and will be most beneficial to:

- ➡ Athletes who want to be considered a team captain prior to being selected or elected

- ➡ Athletes who have been named team captain

- ➡ Team leaders who would like to be a team captain the following year or in another sport

- ➡ Team leaders who want to support their team captain

- ➡ Athletes who want to develop their leadership abilities

Part 3: Extra Steps Section

Anthony Robbins said it best, "Knowledge is not power. Action is power." Simply reading the ideas and strategies presented in this book and not applying them is a waste of time. Each of the pages in the Extra Steps section are perforated so they can easily be torn out from the book if desired.

The Extra Steps section features:

- Workshop notes

- A Certified Team Captain packet featuring written application exercises, reflective journaling pages, forms, surveys, and charts

- A chapter specifically for the parents of athletes

Workshop notes

A set of workshop notes is included in the Extra Steps section. These pages could be used for live leadership work-shops presented at your school by an athletic director or coach. I, or a trainer from my orga-nization, could also use the workshop notes in a live, interactive leader-ship session.

Certified Team Captain Packet

Many schools require athletes seeking a team captain position to become certified by completing various assigned pages from the Extra Steps section. A completed Certification Packet can be submitted to a coach or athletic director as a prerequisite to being considered an official team captain.

The importance of the certification process is that it builds confidence in those athletes taking on the role of team captain. Because the book's content covers essential aspects of team leadership, the certification process helps students internalize and apply the material. The certification process also demonstrates to the team, coaching staff, and athletic administration that a student has put in the necessary time and energy to represent a team as a captain effectively.

Top-notch student-leaders are committed to going beyond what is required as they pursue becoming the best leader possible. The Extra Steps section was created to provide additional structure that will take readers to the next level of leadership.

Parenting for a season of significance

A chapter written specifically for parents is positioned at the end of the Extra Steps section. Leaders will be able to remove this chapter from the book so that parents, stepparents, grandparents, guardians, and other adult family members can gain valuable insight into parenting for a season of significance.

Regardless of your current status, this book provides important points of clarity for leaders and captains who wish to expand their mind and skills.

The leadership lessons from this book will challenge you to rethink or reflect on concepts you may not have thought about in the past.

A Season of Significance

According to Webster's dictionary, the word "significance" is defined as something that is "meaningful, important, and memorable." Success is defined as a "favorable result." Significance is about creating lasting, important memories and lessons, whereas success is about the end result. Ideally, your season and your life will be both significant and successful.

Because this book focuses on a creating a season of significance, I'm often asked, "Are you saying winning is not important?" It's a valid question. Let me be clear. As someone who is very competitive—even with something as simple as a board game—I want to win! Given the choice of winning or losing, I'll take the win. But, it's also important to understand that winning becomes a by-product of hard work and preparation that takes place before and during a sport's season.

Creating a season of significance is challenging

Unfortunately, several things can get in the way of a significant season. When I conduct live workshops, we discuss the issues that can steal away a great experience in high school sports. Students generated the following list when asked to name the top 10 things that prevent a meaningful, important, memorable season.

1. Poor attitude
2. Complaining teammates
3. Injuries
4. Little or no talent
5. Issues with the coach
6. Selfishness
7. Infractions
8. Lack of preparation
9. Bad decisions outside the sport that create drama
10. Poor or no leadership

Look carefully at the list. Teams have some control or influence over eight of the ten items. There are only two items over which teams have little or no control: injuries and talent level.

Injuries can happen to anyone on any time. Many trainers say, however, that getting in strong physical condition, eating right, staying hydrated, and stretching can minimize or prevent injuries.

Regarding talent, with hard work in the off-season and using every resource possible, the team can improve, even if the talent isn't particularly strong. Such work can still create a season of significance. Consider this example:

A good friend of mine was the girls' soccer coach at a large school in central Minnesota. During his first two years, the team only won two games. Despite their record, the team worked hard and improved. Prior to the banquet at the end of the season, a few girls organized an incredible gift for their coach. Each girl was given a 12-inch square piece of fabric. No two pieces of fabric were the same. The girls were asked to write a message with a permanent marker to their coach about what was important and memorable from the season.

As the coach was about to give out awards, the team presented him with a quilt that featured all the pieces of fabric sewn together. Just as each piece of fabric was unique, so was each team member, yet they were bound together by the bond their coach created. One of the girls said to the gathered audience, "Coach, we only won a few games, but we will never forget being a part of this team."

As the coach was sharing this story with me, his voice cracked and tears welled up. He said it was one of the best gifts he's ever been given. Despite their win-loss record, the team had a season of significance.

Let's return to the last item on the top ten things that interfere with a season of significance. *Poor or no leadership.*

There is no longer an excuse for poor or no leadership on a team! By committing yourself and becoming a student of leadership by applying the ideas and concepts here, your team will have confident, competent leaders and captains.

If you are ready and willing to dive into a leadership role and create a season of significance, Chapter 1, "Practicing the Fundamentals," will cover the value of mastering the basics. Let's get started!

Please go to the **Certification Packet** in section three to complete the application exercises for this chapter.

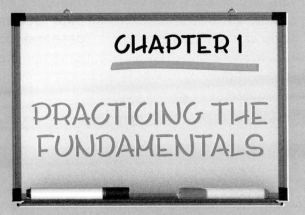

CHAPTER 1

PRACTICING THE FUNDAMENTALS

"If you're not fundamentally strong—you will struggle."
—Corey Kennedy

My wife, Kelly, and I are blessed with two great kids, DJ, the oldest, and Abigayle. Both have been involved in sports from the time they could walk. I was fortunate to coach my son as he played on several summer baseball teams. One particular season, he was doing a great job defensively as a catcher. Offensively, he was in a rut at the plate. His batting average was hovering around 160, and his anxiety about grabbing a bat and entering the batter's box had become very apparent.

It all boiled over when he struck out three consecutive times in one game. As he entered the dugout, he slammed his bat to the ground, looked at me, shook his head, and said angrily, "I STINK!"

As a parent and a coach, I've learned to give the kids and athletes some space in moments like these. He certainly wasn't going to buy into me saying, "No, you're doing all right." And, at that point, he wasn't in the right mindset to hear feedback about why he was struggling. He first needed some time to take in what was happening. Later, we would look at how to improve his performance at the plate.

A few days after the strikeout fiasco, Kelly ran into Mr. Kennedy at a store. Mr. Kennedy was DJ's third grade teacher and a baseball coach who knew a lot about batting. When he asked how DJ's baseball season was going, she shared our son's recent struggle.

As a great coach and teacher, Mr. Kennedy offered to meet DJ at the batting cage and work on his technique. Later that night at dinner, Kelly told DJ about Mr. Kennedy's offer to help with a batting lesson. She was expecting him to say something such as, "That would be awesome!" Instead, we heard, "I don't know. . .maybe." Here was a kid who was offered a great opportunity to improve his baseball skills from someone he knew and admired. Oddly, DJ hesitated. Pride and self-doubt were getting in his way of asking for help.

Do you know someone who would rather cling to false pride and stay in the pit of despair? They often claim they will figure it out on their own, because they don't need anyone telling them what to do. Is it possible that person could be you? Too often, athletes let the fear of looking bad temporarily outweigh the benefits of learning a new skill and climbing out of their rut.

Hearing DJ's lukewarm response, I said, "This is a pretty cool opportunity, but we are not going to make you go. Maybe think about it for a while, and let us know."

What do you think would have happened if we had insisted DJ work with Mr. Kennedy? Most likely, he would have shown up because he had to be there and would have mentally fought the instructions. My experience indicates that when parents or coaches want a result more than the student–athlete wants the result, it's probably not going to happen.

The same thing will be true for the athletes holding this book in their hands. You have an opportunity to read this book, apply the strategies presented, and leap into leadership. *Unfortunately, there are always students who attend one of my workshops or who are asked to read a book on leadership and are less than thrilled about the opportunity. Rather than becoming inspired by the material and applying the content, they ignore it.*

> **When parents or coaches want a result more than the student-athlete wants the result, it's probably not going to happen.**

The next morning at breakfast DJ said, "I've been thinking about the batting lesson, and I want to set it up." His decision to pursue the lessons indicated he was willing to break down what was going wrong and eventually break through to become a better hitter. *Break Down—Break Through!*

When we arrived at the batting cage, DJ's anxiety was evident. Coach Kennedy started with questions. "What do you think about when you walk up to the plate?" he asked.

My son responded, "I hope I don't strike out."

"Ok," said Coach Kennedy. "The first thing we need to work on is your mental approach. Rather than walking up to the plate hoping not to strike out, I want you to simply be present."

This threw DJ off. "What does that mean? Be present?"

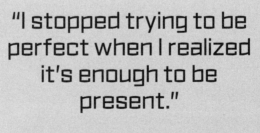

"I stopped trying to be perfect when I realized it's enough to be present."

–Curtis Tyrone Jones

Mr. Kennedy explained, "You can't control what happened in the last game or for that matter the last time you were at bat. But you do have some control on the *right now*," he said. "When you walk up to the plate, commit to being in the moment. Say to yourself, 'Whatever he throws at me, I can hit. I got this!'"

DJ responded, "Yeah, but I haven't been hitting at all!"

"Well then, what do you have to lose by changing your approach?" Kennedy asked.

Something in DJ's eyes lit up, and he started to get the message on how he was approaching the batter's box.

"Let's start over here," said Mr. Kennedy as he walked over to a baseball tee that had a ball on top of it. The confusion on DJ's face made me laugh. Apparently, he couldn't keep his thoughts to himself as he said, "I'm a baseball player, not a tee-ball player!"

Coach Kennedy let those words sit in the air for a while and then he made a statement that became embedded in my son's brain for the rest of his athletic career and his current career as a personal trainer.

Kennedy said, "If you are not fundamentally sound, you will struggle."

These simple, yet powerful words are at the core for anyone in a performance role. Too often as we age and develop in a sport or even a career, we drift from the fundamentals. Often this happens because we think we are beyond the mundane skills that players do when first learning a sport. Think of how many athletes complain about the first few weeks of practice. Athletes moan and groan about the tedious drills, uncomfortable conditioning, and repeating simple skills that have been done and supposedly mastered in elementary school. Then think about a team that is not conditioned and starts to make poor decisions because they are tired. During a competition, have you ever seen a teammate mess up something that is considered simple? When we start to focus on finesse instead of fundamentals, we are positioning ourselves to fail. As a leader, never consider yourself to be too good to be fundamentally strong.

After DJ realized the importance of starting with the fundamentals, he was asked to demonstrate how he bats in a game. This would help Coach Kennedy diagnose the issues. DJ gripped the bat as tight as he could and took a few monster swings at the tee. The sound of the tee being struck and seeing the short distance the ball traveled indicated his technique was poor. Coach Kennedy then asked me to video each batting attempt for the next game.

Many times athletes benefit from watching their performance on video. It can be very humbling watching your performance on screen. Although you think you look one way, the video might show something totally different. Yet, the camera doesn't lie. Video feedback can be one of the most valuable tools for athletes provided they are open to getting feedback and watching their performance to look for ways to improve. With technological advancements, it's not uncommon for athletes to watch themselves seconds after a performance. When you are willing to evaluate yourself on video, the odds of correcting a situation increase dramatically and quickly. Be wise enough to embrace the feedback instead of rejecting it with an excuse.

After watching DJ take several cuts at the ball on a tee Coach Kennedy said, "Let's make a few adjustments and see if we can get you hitting like you are capable of hitting." The coach started working on hand placement, footwork, timing, and how to watch the ball being released from the pitcher's hand.

> Be wise enough to embrace feedback instead of rejecting it with an excuse.

It's always interesting to watch and listen to a coach provide instruction to athletes. I'm intrigued by the words used, tone of voice, and body language displayed when giving feedback. Coach Kennedy used the word "adjust" instead of "change," which is easier to digest mentally. (You will learn more about the language of leaders in chapter 19.) His tone of voice was more encouraging than confrontational. Finally, his body language indicated he was tuned in to his student and wanted him to improve. The subtle awareness of our words, tone of voice, and body language can be the difference between someone getting the message or giving up.

It was a bit painful to watch the first 30 minutes of DJ's lesson. For a time, DJ was actually doing worse than when he first started. After the first lesson, DJ said there was a time when he thought he was never going to get better.

Anytime we are unlearning old habits and trying to learn new ones, it's going to be awkward. Brain memory and muscle memory can override a new technique. We can easily revert to what we're doing. It is beneficial to establish a realistic time frame when making a change in life. Many experts say it takes 21 days to create a new habit or break a habit that is no longer desirable.

It takes 21 days to create a new habit or break a habit.

About 40 minutes into the lesson, something clicked for my son. The adjustments he was so conscious about trying to adopt now looked more natural. It was as if I could visually see him move from the *Awakening* season to the *Strengthening* season you will learn about in Chapter 2. Then, he hit a ball farther than he had ever hit before. All three of us smiled and celebrated. Even though it was just one hit, the awkward nature of the initial part of the lesson was overshadowed by new success.

Usually the sacrifice to reach a goal evaporates once the goal is attained. Ask any woman who has given birth about this concept. Almost all will reply, "It was painful, but now that the baby is here, it was all worth it." The same principle is true in life and sports. The uncomfortable feelings of learning something new dissipate when the goal is attained. The key is to trust the process and be willing to go through the initial steps of unlearning and relearning to reach a new level.

DJ's team had two back-to-back games a few days after his initial batting lesson. He got a hit 7 of his 8 times at the plate. His confidence was apparent each time he stepped into the batter's box. His new approach played a role in his performance, and the smile on his face said it all. On the drive home, he said, "Dad—those small adjustments made a big difference!"

It's amazing to see how small adjustments, good or bad, over a period of time, can impact a person's performance. By simply making a few changes, DJ's performance at the plate was dramatically better. Great athletes are always searching for those slight changes to improve in their sport.

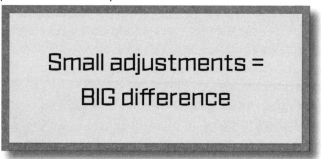

Small adjustments =
BIG difference

Something common, but disappointing, happened at DJ's next game. The confidence he had from the previous game now bordered on arrogance. DJ went one for four at the plate. Why did this happen? Two things messed him up. First, he was guilty of believing the last performance would equal the next performance. Second, he either forgot or thought he no longer needed to use some of the strategies Coach Kennedy had taught him at the first meeting.

DJ's experience is a reminder to approach each practice or performance in a humble fashion and remember that last week's game has little to do with this week's game. We need to be wise enough to begin at ground zero. By taking this approach, we are setting ourselves up to perform at our best for that game, regardless of what happened at previous games.

Rather than sulking about his poor performance, DJ asked us when he could take another lesson from Coach Kennedy. It was as if he realized the importance of reviewing and renewing his skills. To make a long story short, he took several more lessons and ended the season batting over 500. It was a strong finish to a season that started off poorly.

Past ≠ Future

"When I was young, I had to learn the fundamentals of basketball. You can have all the physical ability in the world, but you still have to know the fundamentals."

— Michael Jordan

Looking back, the season taught all of us a lot more about life in general than playing baseball. Some of the lessons include:

- Seek wisdom from coaches

- Battle through tough times

- Put pride aside

- Be present in the moment

- Approach each situation with an open mind

- Understand that awkwardness is a part of the learning process

I hope by now you have figured out that this book is not just about leading a team to a season of significance. It's also about leading a life of significance.

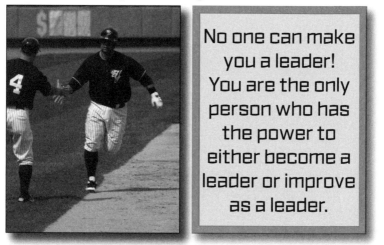

No one can make you a leader! You are the only person who has the power to either become a leader or improve as a leader.

Please go to the **Certification Packet** in section three to complete the application exercises for this chapter.

CHAPTER 2

EMBRACING THE SEASONS OF LEADERSHIP

"Good seasons start with good beginnings."
— Sparky Anderson, former professional baseball manager

A year is divided into four seasons. In my home state of Minnesota, the seasons are all remarkably different; in other parts of the country and world, there are few, if any, changes to the weather. Still, all kinds of transitions occur when one season ends and another begins.

Just as there are seasons in a year, there are also seasons of leadership. Janet Hagberg and Robert A. Guelich, authors of *The Critical Journey*, introduce the concept of the "stages of life." Their concepts address seasons of leadership. The metaphor has had a profound effect on my perspective regarding the process and cycles leaders must understand as they embark on and continue their leadership journey.

The seasons of leadership

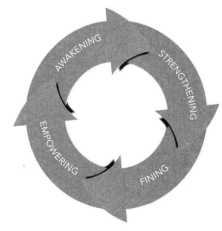

Awakening: Leaders in the awakening season begin to realize they have an internal desire to lead. It's also possible someone else has expressed to an awakening leader that they have leadership potential. It's common for people in this season to randomly put themselves in leadership roles. They may volunteer to handle a small commitment. Essentially, they are putting their toes in the waters of leadership.

Strengthening: After a person becomes aware they have leadership potential, it's common to pursue more opportunities that might have been previously ignored. The strengthening season features more initiative such as signing up for committees and exploring resources including books, online articles, and videos that provide instruction and motivation for becoming better. People in the strengthening season seem to have a thirst for new knowledge, and they are excited about applying the new knowledge.

Refining: During the refining process, a leader makes small, subtle changes that improve her capabilities. At times, this season can be a struggle. The initial growth experienced from the strengthening season slows down, and getting to the next level requires new strategies. Let's look at lifting weights as an example of how the  refining season works. Assume someone starts with a test to determine the maximum amount he or she can bench press. This establishes a starting point. By bench-pressing three times a week for ten weeks, there will be a noticeable improvement in the amount of weight they can now lift. The percentage increase over the next ten weeks, however, is rarely the same as it was during the first ten weeks. The rate of improvement is smaller, even with the same lifting schedule. Too often, people get frustrated, because they are not increasing their strength as quickly as they did during the first ten weeks of training. The refining season often requires people to fine tune their approach and understand that even though improvement seems slower, they are still improving.

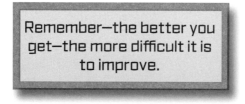

Remember—the better you get—the more difficult it is to improve.

Empowering: When people are more concerned about helping others than themselves, they have moved into the empowering season of leadership. This is the ultimate season. Few people enter this season, because it's easy to get caught up in the power and glory that leadership sometimes provides. Empowering leaders harvest all the wisdom from the first three seasons and help or empower others to become their best.

Empowering is similar to running in a relay race in the sport of track. Each member of the team carries a baton with the goal of running his/her best leg of the race. At the end of each leg, the baton is handed off to the next runner, who is now empowered to run the next portion of the race. Most leaders agree that there is no greater feeling than empowering someone else to excel to the next stage of life or leadership. Leaders who are blessed enough to enter this season live a life of significance. They know deep down they made a difference in someone else's life and in the world.

The seasons of leadership are cyclical and evolving. Each time you approach a new stage in life, the seasons reemerge. Think back to kindergarten. A parent introduces the awakening season by getting you out of bed one morning and telling you it's the first day of school. You arrive at school feeling somewhat scared about saying goodbye to the world as you know it and entering the world of education.

After working through the uncomfortable awakening season, you start to get in a groove and felt stronger about your capabilities as you enter into the strengthening season. At some point, school transforms from a lot of fun and games to actually learning new things. Maybe you struggled with reading and found the refining process difficult. Finally, if your school held a preview for next year's kindergarten class, you had the chance to be in the empowering season. By walking a future student around the room and easing their fears, you learned the incredible feeling of helping another person.

> "There are seasons in life. Don't ever let anyone try to deny you the joy of one season because they believe you should stay in another season. Listen to yourself. Trust you instincts. Keep your perspective." — Jane Clayson

Of course, as you entered first grade, the seasons all lined up again. The good and bad news is the seasons never stop evolving. Life is one adventure after another!

Often, we want to race through the seasons instead of enjoying each season. Although it's important to strive and grow, when we understand the seasons and embrace our position in each season, we can truly enjoy the leadership journey.

So, enjoy whatever season you are currently experiencing. There is beauty, growth potential, and excitement in each season.

Please go to the *Certification Packet* in section three to complete the application exercises for this chapter.

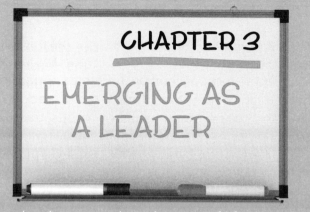

CHAPTER 3

EMERGING AS A LEADER

"High school sports: where lessons of life are still being learned and where athletes still compete for the love of the game and their teammates." — Michael Powers

When you are first learning how to drive, merging can make you nervous. Let's agree: merging into traffic is tricky. You must know the power of your vehicle while estimating the speed of others. Merging also requires awareness of vehicles behind you, ahead of you, and beside you. Furthermore, there's road construction, detours, and accidents complicating the picture. To top it off, traffic dynamics are always changing, because other drivers are making decisions as well. Even seasoned drivers can become uneasy when merging in a high traffic area that is new or unfamiliar. Merging, however, is necessary. It usually allows traffic to keep flowing.

Team leaders must learn how to merge with coaches, teammates, and other team leaders. But like driving, merging with others as a team can be complex, frustrating, and nerve racking if not done properly.

Emerging is derived from merge.
Merge means to come forth into view or notice; to develop.

You or someone you know believes you have leadership qualities. To help pinpoint the most important leadership qualities, I surveyed coaches and athletes regarding the personal qualities they look for in team leaders. After compiling and condensing the survey results, ten qualities emerged.

By embracing and displaying the following ten qualities described in this chapter, you are on your way to maximizing your strength as a leader and inspiring others to merge with you on the road to a season of significance. The certification packet in section 3 provides a way to help you gauge yourself on each of the qualities.

There are additional qualities leaders possess beyond the ten covered in this chapter. Chapter 19, *Shifting into the Team Captain Role*, featured in the *team captain* section of the book, describes the next level qualities for elected team captains. Before diving into the personality qualities, let me clarify the difference between a quality and a skill.

Qualities versus Skills

There is a difference between a *quality* and a *skill*. Both can be developed over time, but they are measured in different ways.

Qualities are related to a person's personality and are revealed or tested in real-world situations. Qualities are difficult to measure, because they are subjective. Qualities can also be perceptual. For example, a classmate who has a quality of being humorous may be considered hilarious by the class. The teacher, however, may view the same individual as someone who distracts the class by blurting out inappropriate comments at the wrong time.

A skill, in contrast, can be learned through a series of instructions and is measured by results. Skills could be physical or mental. For example, a softball pitcher can learn the skills required to throw a curve ball. Resolving conflict is a mental skill that can be practiced and used during a disagreement.

To be effective, great leaders must develop both qualities and skills.

When a person possesses certain qualities, learning new skills occurs more quickly. For example, a gymnast, with the quality of determination, will master a full twist faster  than a teammate who gives up as soon as she can't do a layout. To be considered a leader, you must demonstrate vital qualities while also pursuing various skills.

Qualities enhance skills

Top 10 qualities of emerging team leaders

Quality # 1 Trust

David Horsager, author of *The Trust Edge*, asks his readers to think about an important event: "Describe a time when you were totally trusted by someone." I thought back to a family vacation we took to a resort in northern Minnesota. At the time DJ was five, and Abigayle was two. Abigayle loved being in the pool but could not swim. I was in the pool where the depth was five feet and Abigayle was standing on the pool's deck, about two feet from the pool's edge. The video clip shows me encouraging her to leap to me in the water. Even though she was young, she was aware of how deep the pool was and she wasn't wearing any type of floating device.

Abigayle hesitated for a minute and then took two big steps and leapt into the pool where I caught her. The smile on her face was priceless! Do you think she would have jumped into the pool if she didn't trust me? No chance!

How trustworthy are you?

After a coach walks out of the door, do you mock or criticize her? If someone on your team shares some confidential family information, do you spread it to the rest of the team or post it on social media?

Being trustworthy is about integrity, faithfulness, devotion, responsibility, and respect. It means keeping information confidential. If someone confides in you and asks you to keep a secret, you're being trustworthy if you don't tell anyone else—not even your best friend. Trustworthy team leaders may know a lot about people that is not public information, but they don't spread it around. And a common saying about trust states: Trust takes years to build, seconds to break, and forever to repair. I think this speaks for itself.

Trust takes years to build, seconds to break, and forever to repair.

Now, there are a few times when you shouldn't keep a secret. If someone shares information about hurting him or herself—or hurting others—you must tell someone who can help. Who do you tell? A trustworthy adult. That person could be a coach, a teacher, a parent, or a counselor. A trustworthy adult will know what to do.

So what about you? Can you keep information confidential when it won't be harmful to others? When there is a threat of someone being hurt, do you feel comfortable communicating the issue with an adult? If so, teammates will be pulled to you like a magnet because they know you will be there 100% of the time. When people trust you, they will listen and follow you.

Quality # 2 Passion

"Passion is energy. Feel the power that comes from focusing on what excites you." — Oprah Winfrey

Passion is like a magnet. It has the ability to pull people in and create a bond that fosters excitement and energy to learn something new, attain a goal, or find a purpose. Think of a teacher who is passionate about her subject. Even if you don't share that passion, you at least admire how she is fired up about seeing students learn the material. You also may have had classes where the instructor had lost her passion. Because the instructor didn't seem to care, the odds are that most students didn't care either. Do you want to be connected to someone who is disconnected from the people she is leading?

In sports, passionate leaders have a zeal for the sport. They want to improve their abilities and often make the extra effort to attend camps, watch instructional videos, and study other athletes who may be performing at a higher level. Athletes who have genuine passion and enthusiasm toward life and their sport create a magnetic pull that can motivate teammates to dig deeper and reach new levels.

Unfortunately, passion can be overdone. Assume someone loves to work out by lifting weights. If all they can talk about is their workout plan and how much weight they can lift, people will soon grow tired of this conversation.

Great team leaders show their enthusiasm for the sport at the appropriate times. They also have the ability to dial it down and have conversations that include others who can share their own passions about sports or life.

Quality # 3 Strong Work Ethic

"There may be people who have more talent than you, but there's no excuse for anyone to work harder than you do." — Derek Jeter

My best friend and speaking colleague, Bill Cordes, wrote the YOGOWYPI book. YOGOWYPI stands for "You only get out what you put in." Too often, people of all ages want to figure out a way to get more out than what they put in. Think about a teammate who is constantly complaining about lack of playing time, yet rarely arrives early or stays late for practice.

A young man named Mitch that I knew understands the YOGOWYPI concept. He is one of the hardest working athletes I have ever been around. As a 7th grader, he was a lanky kid who found himself as the backup to the backup quarterback. Growing up, he was not the most talented kid on the team; however, he was unquestionably known as the hardest worker on every team in every situation. Whether it was a conditioning drill or running the scout offense as a sophomore, he would often say, "No one will outwork me."

As a junior, the compound effect of his hard work started to pay off. His commitment to improving his agility, first step explosion, and speed in the off-season took him from the backup position to the starting quarterback at one of the top high schools in Minnesota. I asked his head coach to list his leadership qualities for this book. The first quality I heard was, "The kid works harder than anyone else, and he creates a climate where his teammates are inspired to do the same."

Not only did Mitch want to be considered a great high school quarterback, he wanted to play at the University of Minnesota. The dream became a reality as he was named the starting quarterback entering his sophomore year. The *Star Tribune* newspaper featured an article on Mitch as he was entering the second year as the starter. Most of the article focused on his work ethic and the amount of time he invested preparing himself and his teammates during the off-season and during the week prior to a game.

It would have been easier to be satisfied with being an above average high school athlete. Instead, Mitch L. became a living example of the YOGOWPI principle.

It's been said that, "Hard work beats talent when talent doesn't work hard." When you are one of the hardest workers on the team, you eventually become your best. Working hard creates a climate that allows everyone on the team to reach their potential.

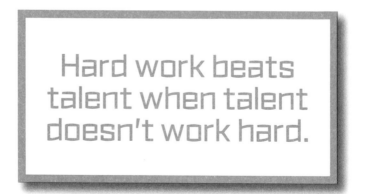

Hard work beats talent when talent doesn't work hard.

Quality # 4 Resilience

Imagine being on a team that didn't win a single game in four years. Think about how difficult it would be to get athletes to even come out for the sport with a history of 84 losses in a row.

That's the story of a girls' basketball team from northern Minnesota. While attempting to end the losing streak of 84 games, fouls mounted so high that the last three minutes and six seconds of the game were played three players against five players. No one could dream up such a difficult situation! Despite the odds of winning being impossible, the three girls on the floor showed remarkable resilience. The remaining three girls won the game in double overtime by four points and broke the 84 game losing streak!

Resilience is our ability to bounce back when the future appears gloomy or uncertain. It may be helpful to look at the word resilience with a creative eye. What if we see "re-silence?" Often, we need to "re-silence" the internal voice of doubt that too often rules our lives. By consistently silencing mental doubt during uncertainty in life or sports, we put ourselves in a better position to turn things around and reach the goal we were pursuing.

The article that covered the basketball story was very inspiring. One of the girls said, "We just had to give it of our heart and desire. We couldn't stop. We didn't have a choice." Another girl stated, "Obviously, it's not enjoyable to lose. When you're in that kind of streak, you find other things to get excited about like winning a half or the first four minutes or team chemistry and relationships."

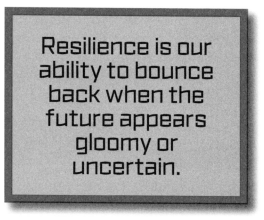

Resilience is our ability to bounce back when the future appears gloomy or uncertain.

This is a remarkable story of being resilient and bouncing back. The girls could have easily thought the losing streak would continue. Instead, they shut down the voice of doubt, looked for small victories in the game, and ended up with a win. As a footnote, the resilient hoops team won four additional games that year.

Quality # 5 Integrity

As an 8th grade track participant, I was recruited to be the line judge for the long jump event for a varsity track meet. My job was to watch the line, and if a jumper's foot touched or went over the line, I was to yell out "scratch." A scratch jump is invalid.

Our varsity team had an incredible jumper who consistently took first place in this event. After two jumps, T.S. was in third place. On his final approach, he clearly stepped over the line, so I yelled "scratch." For some reason, the official didn't hear me, and the jump was measured. As the official announced, "22 feet, 6 inches," I approached the official and said it was a scratch jump. The official apologized for not hearing me and announced the jump wouldn't count. Little did I know that 22'6" would have been a new school record. I was simply doing the job I was asked to do.

The next thing I knew, T.S. was in my face. He verbally tore into me. "You just cost me the school record, punk!" he yelled. "Why did you do that?" (That is the edited version of what he said.) I was totally caught off-guard and found myself almost speechless. The only thing I could say was, "You scratched. You went over the line."

That experience has been etched in my mind ever since that encounter. T.S. wanted to have his name on the record board despite the fact he didn't even earn the honor. Talk about dishonesty! In an instant, I went from a young athlete who totally admired his athletic ability to an athlete who was disgusted by his lack of integrity.

Arthur Calwel once said, "It is better to be defeated on principle, than to win on lies." If you are going to be considered a team leader, you have to be honest and have integrity when people are watching — and perhaps more importantly, when no one is watching.

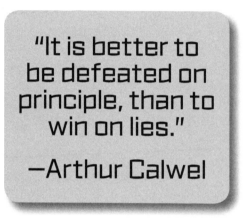

"It is better to be defeated on principle, than to win on lies."

—Arthur Calwel

Quality # 6 Coachability

In one of my leadership programs, I begin to juggle three tennis balls. After I demonstrate the skill for a short time, the audience hears they will now have the opportunity to learn to

> "If you are not willing to learn, no one can help you. If you are determined to learn, no one can stop you."
> – Zig Ziglar

juggle. (Students who have already mastered juggling become my assistant coaches.) Once the audience hears about the challenge, they find a partner from whom they will receive coaching and take on the role as coach themselves. Students then write down their attitude, thoughts and internal dialogue regarding juggling. All three pieces—attitude, thoughts, and self-talk/internal dialogue—create their approach. It's fascinating for students to see the changes in all three areas as they tackle a new skill. Normally, the way they approach juggling is similar to how they approach learning anything else.

Students are invited to share their attitude with the group before any specific instructions are given. The comments are very telling about their approach. Some students say, "I have always wanted to learn how to juggle—bring it on." Others say, "I have tried before, and I can't." Some roll their eyes and ask, "What's the point?"

CQ = Approach + Focused Attention + Follow-through

> Most people believe someone's success in life will be determined by their IQ or "Intelligence Quotient." I believe success can be determined by someone's CQ or "Coachability Quotient." — Craig Hillier

The juggling activity gives the participants a glimpse of a leader's Coachability Quotient.

Approach: Did the student have an open mind to learn juggling? Did they get down on themselves when it became difficult or did they mentally reset and begin again? What did their internal dialogue reveal regarding their self-talk?

Focused Attention: Did the student listen to the specific instructions during each phase of the activity or was listening selective? Did they listen to their partner during the short feedback sessions, or did they become stubborn and insist on doing things their way?

Follow-through: Did the students follow through on the feedback they received from me or from their partner by changing and adjusting? It's interesting that other people can see issues we either ignore or aren't willing to see.

Consistently, I find the students who have a high CQ learn to juggle in 60 minutes or less. Those with a low CQ normally struggle with learning to juggle and say they didn't like the activity on the evaluation—which isn't much of a surprise.

Quality # 7 Flexibility

Let's assume you have played a certain position on a team since middle school. Now the coach is asking you to play a different position. Maybe a teammate has improved immensely in the off-season and suddenly that player is getting more playing time than you. Maybe a new student moves to your school who has great talent and will make a strong contribution to the team.

How do you respond? Are you flexible enough to give the new position a try? Or do you become stubborn and refuse to adapt?

Flexibility is a must for team leaders. It demonstrates you are willing to put the team's needs in front of your own. This doesn't happen without some internal pain, because you may look awkward and feel uncomfortable learning the new position. Sometimes you will have to put your pride aside and look at the big picture.

The flexible leader may surprise himself when challenged to take on a new position. It's very possible the new position could be a better fit than the original position, provided the right mind-set is in place.

Flexibility can also be demonstrated in competition. There may be times when an entire new game plan will be introduced a few days before a competition or even during a break in the game. The ability to adjust and adapt from one situation to another is vital for top-notch leaders.

Quality # 8 Accountable

When applying for a business expansion loan, the accounting department prepares a balance sheet. This document is a snapshot of a company's financial position as of a specified date. A balance sheet that shows low assets (income) and high liabilities (bills) rarely gets approved. However, loaning institutions that see a balance sheet showing high assets and low liabilities will likely extend credit through a loan.

Coaches and teammates have a mental balance sheet on leadership ability. If you are a leader who brings a lot of assets to the team—by demonstrating the other qualities in this chapter—coaches and teammates will credit you as a leader. Conversely, athletes who bring more liabilities to the team won't have the creditability to be considered a leader.

Practice and game day balance sheet for Y O U

Assets	Liabilities
Shows up early	Shows up slightly late
Prepared	Unprepared
Acknowledges mistakes	Blames mistakes on others
Wants to improve	Content with current skill level
All-out effort	Plays hard when they "feel like it"
Joyful spirit	Moody and unpredictable
Unselfish	Selfish
"Tuned in" to coaches and teammates	"Tuned out" to coaches and teammates

Does your personal balance sheet show more assets or liabilities? Will your coaches and teammates credit you as a team leader based on your balance sheet?

Quality # 9 Confidence

There is a thin line between confidence and arrogance. While the line is thin, the results are not.

In a leadership training session, when I ask students what they would like to work on, several athletes invariably choose the topic of confidence. While I

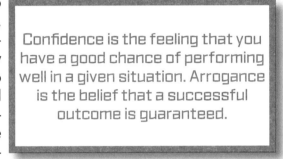

Confidence is the feeling that you have a good chance of performing well in a given situation. Arrogance is the belief that a successful outcome is guaranteed.

can't give you confidence, I can tell you how to get confidence. There are four steps to gaining confidence as an individual and as a team leader.

Step A: Recognize that you're afraid to look awkward.

If you've ever driven a car with a manual transmission, you know what I'm talking about. You shift from one gear to the next while pushing in the clutch with no effort or thought. Most people think, "It looks easy, but there's no way I'm trying that. I'd look like an idiot if I tried."

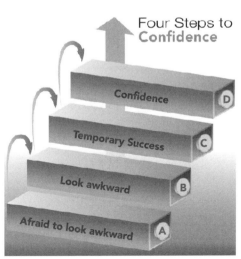

Four Steps to Confidence

Confidence — D
Temporary Success — C
Look awkward — B
Afraid to look awkward — A

It's the fear of looking bad that holds most of us back from reaching our true potential. Sometimes, we don't even try because our fears are so overpowering.

Then someone encourages you to give it a try. That person usually remembers what it was like to learn. Maybe she says, "Oh, you'll probably kill the engine. Sometimes, you'll feel like you're riding a wild horse, but that happened to me. You'll get the hang of it after you try it a few times."

As soon as you get into the driver's seat, you're overcoming your fear and preparing for step two. As soon as you let out the clutch the first time, you're on to step two.

Step B: Look awkward!

When you let the clutch out, the car shook wildly and probably stopped. Then your friend or parent gave you a dicey stare, and you gave it another try. Ten minutes later, you were out of the driveway and onto the street. You still probably looked a little foolish, but at least you were going from first gear to second gear instead of from first to fourth. Now you're at step C.

> "Optimism is the faith that leads to achievement. Nothing can be done without hope and confidence." – Helen Keller

Step C: Reach temporary success.

This step feels uncomfortable because you're totally concentrating on what you're doing. Sometimes you find temporary success shifting from one gear to the next and sometimes it feels like you have the new skill down pat. Yet a few minutes later, it feels like you are at the starting point—again as the car stops because you let the clutch out too fast. After persisting for several hours or days of practice with a capable teacher, you're approaching step four.

Step D: Confidence through repetition.

When you reach this step, you know mastering the new skill is possible as you have occasionally or even accidently found success. Repeating what you learned over time inspires the awesome feeling of confidence. But recognize, confidence doesn't just happen in an instant—it only is created through repetition over time.

After you master one skill, you must go through the same four steps the next time to learn something new. You go back to the fear of looking awkward, which doesn't feel good. But that's how you make progress. Whether it's driving a car with a manual transmission or learning a new skill in your sport, you will go through all four steps. Get through step one and two as fast as you can so you can accelerate your progress. How do you get confidence? Experience. How do you get experience? By messing up, learning something important, and then applying the wisdom you gained in the next situation.

Quality # 10 Caring

Very few people willingly follow a leader who doesn't genuinely care about others. When a group senses a leader truly cares about the team and the season, however, they will be willing to outwork and outperform their competition.

In my first book, *How to Step Up as a Teen Leader and Still Keep Your Friends*, I outlined a formula that has been effective for thousands of teen leaders. By using this formula—called CARE—you will create a positive environment with your teammates and coaches.

Compliment. Great leaders are quick to compliment and slow to criticize. When you see a player have a breakthrough, try to be the first one to congratulate her. Most people let their ego or petty jealousy get in the way of giving compliments. Make sure your compliments are honest, sincere, and given out frequently and freely. Ensure you are not fishing for a reciprocal compliment.

Act in the team's best interest. It's easy to get caught up in thinking about "me" instead of "we." One thing is certain, when "me" becomes more important than "we," you and your team will struggle. Sacrifice for the good of the team, and you will see others do the same.

Respect differences in others. Most of us should realistically admit to judging someone before we really knew them. Then, after spending some time with the person, we found our initial judgment was way off base or unfair. The lesson is simple: don't judge until you really know a person. Even after you know someone, be wise enough to withhold judgment and attempt to accept people for who they are, not who you think they should be. Unfortunately, our world is filled with narrow-minded people who judge others by their life circumstances or ethnicity. Even when you respect the differences in others, you may find people who don't respect you or your teammates. When this happens, it's tempting to become judgmental. But realistically, you just see things differently. Treat others with respect even if others are not reciprocal.

Extend a helping hand. Is one of your teammates struggling with a slap shot or hurdling technique? Is someone in your neighborhood trying to learn the sport you play? Take the time to extend a helping hand. Every day you 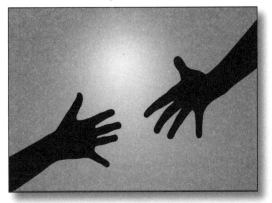 have an opportunity to extend a helping hand. Identify those opportunities and stretch yourself to help. There is no greater feeling in the world than helping someone who needs help.

This CARE formula works wonders. I received an email from a young man who attended one of my leadership programs as a sophomore. He wrote this formula down and committed to using it every day of his life. After using the formula daily, he decided to run for student body president. The school he attended had 2,200 students in grades 10 through 12. When the results were tallied, this young man received 70% of the votes. It was the largest landslide victory in the school's history. As his email stated, he never would have been able to get that many votes without using the CARE formula and making it second nature.

It's now time for you to gauge yourself on the top ten qualities of team leaders. **Please go to the Certification Packet in section 3.** Even if the *Certification Packet* is not required by a coach or athletic director, the assessment will help you gauge the qualities you possess and the qualities you need to develop as a team leader.

> "Never believe that a few caring people can't change the world. For, indeed, that's all who ever have."
> — Margaret Mead

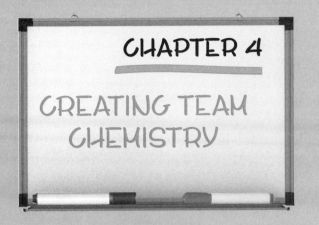

CHAPTER 4

CREATING TEAM CHEMISTRY

"Good teams become great ones when the members trust each other enough to surrender the "me" for the "we." — Phil Jackson

Great chemists understand that when elements are combined, something greater than the individual parts can be created. Combine gas with a spark, you create a fire. Mix hydrogen with oxygen, you get water. Combine baking soda with vinegar, and you have a miniature volcano.

> When elements are combined, they make something new - something that would not exist if each element stayed in its original form.

It's fascinating to listen to coaches being interviewed after the season. If the season was disappointing, you'll hear something like, "The chemistry just wasn't there." Contrast that with a season of significance where coaches say, "Our team chemistry was tremendous."

Let's look at another example. Before gasoline engines were invented, farmers would take their strongest horse and see how much weight it could pull on a sled placed on grass. At one county fair, the first-place horse pulled 1,000 pounds, and the second-place horse pulled 850 pounds. The farmers began to wonder how much the two horses could pull togeth-er. Logic would say 1,850 pounds. Yet when the horses were put together, they pulled 2,500 pounds. It was the combination of the two that allowed them to pull that much weight.

The two principles also apply to great teamwork. As an individual you're limited. And, if you're going to have a season of sig-nificance, you won't do it by yourself. But, by joining together to form a team, you can create something sig-nificant.

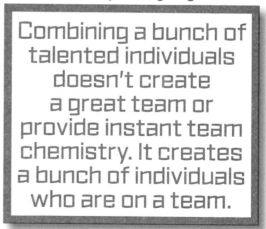

Combining a bunch of talented individuals doesn't create a great team or provide instant team chemistry. It creates a bunch of individuals who are on a team.

Most coaches would rather coach a team with average talent and strong chemistry than a bunch of highly talented individuals who are only concerned about individual accomplishments.

> "A common mistake among those who work in sports is spending a disproportional amount of time on the Xs and Os as compared to time spent learning about people."
> — Mike Krzyzewski, Coach "K"

➡ Team chemistry is created and measured by balancing relationships and tasks.

➡ If there is a consistent emphasis on only one aspect of the team chemistry, the imbalance creates problems.

➡ Relationships form the bond among teammates and the coaching staff. Working relationships in athletics are formed by time spent with each other inside and outside the sport.

➡ Tasks can be defined as the day-to-day physical aspects of sports such as practice, conditioning, meetings, and games or competitions.

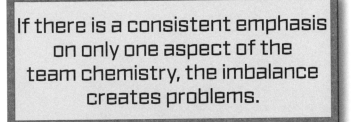

If there is a consistent emphasis on only one aspect of the team chemistry, the imbalance creates problems.

When relationships outweigh tasks

If a team is focused more on relationships than tasks, they will be very close with each other. However, because they are so tight with one another, it's common for teammates to stay silent rather than challenging teammates who are not putting forth maximum effort. The fear is that a confrontation may hurt a teammate's feelings. But in this situation, the team doesn't perform to its potential because of an unspoken resentment toward someone who is not working hard. In addition, if other teammates match the effort of those who are not working hard, the team will struggle against a tough

opponent. In this scenario, preparation just isn't solid.

When tasks outweigh relationships

If tasks are emphasized over relationships, however, team chemistry is strained. When the season is all about "getting the job done" in practice or competition and the focus is only on attaining the next victory, teammates  do not bond well. This approach can lead to sabotaging teammates to get a leg up on another player. For example, rather than inviting everyone on the team to attend a camp or program, individuals attend by themselves with the goal of learning something that will increase their playing time. When coaches focus solely on tasks and don't seem to care about relationships, sports can become a daily grind. Yet, the number one reason athletes participate at the high school level is to have fun. When the fun is missing, a team may have a strong win–loss record, but the joy of participating diminishes, leading to a season of INsignificance.

The team chemistry scale is constantly fluctuating. There will be times, especially in the off-season, where relationships may outweigh tasks. Toward the end of a season as the team is preparing for the playoffs, tasks may outweigh relationships. When relationships have been forged prior to and throughout the season, a coaching staff and team can shift into task mode. A team responds well in this situation because relationships have been solidified earlier in the year.

In addition to balancing tasks and relationships, it's also important to understand the five stages of team chemistry.

Stages of Team Chemistry

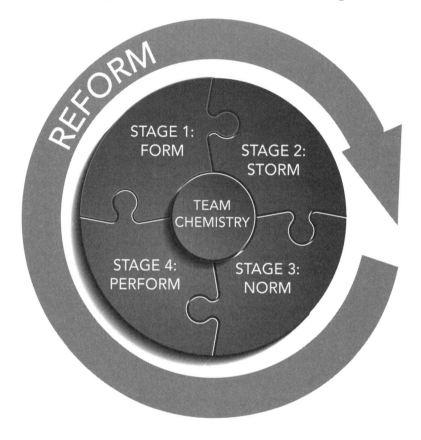

Stage 1: Form Depending on the sport, a team can be in this stage immediately after one season ends and the junior class becomes the senior class. If a team is created through a try-out process, the form stage occurs after the team is announced.

The form stage can be a little awkward as the team is getting comfortable with new teammates or getting comfortable being a year older. For example, a sophomore player who was on the JV team is now on a varsity squad as a junior. This takes some mental adjusting.

The form stage creates an excellent opportunity to connect with everyone who is new to the team. If a new coach has been hired, this is also a key time to connect with her. During this time, leaders should focus on building relationships. The form stage is less stressful when teammates are sincerely interested in learning about one another. As a leader, this is your chance to find the common denominator with others by asking a variety of questions to break the ice and begin to create unity. You can ask questions that pertain to sports and questions unrelated to sports. The point is to get athletes talking and sharing.

It's important to connect with all of your teammates during the form stage. Too often, we connect with just a handful of players with whom we have a history and exclude or ignore teammates we either don't know or with whom we've perhaps had a difficult past situation. If we don't connect with everyone, cliques start to form, and creating team chemistry can become very difficult.

Find the common denominator with your teammates.

Stage 2: Storm The storm stage is the most crucial and unpredictable phase of team chemistry. Maybe you have experienced a day during which a rainstorm seemingly came out of nowhere. You may have also experienced a day that starts with a rainstorm, but by mid-morning the storm has passed and the sky is clear. Every team will experience storms. Some storms last a few minutes, whereas others can last an entire season.

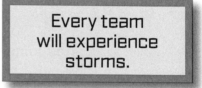

The unpredictable nature of storms can cause issues with team chemistry if they are not handled properly. A team can face two types of storms, healthy and toxic.

Healthy storming occurs when teammates and coaches can discuss and even disagree with each other on a variety of topics without fear of resentment or anger. For example, a coach may ask a team with other coaches present, "What could we—coaches and players—have done differently at our last game?" If the coaching staff and team can contribute candid feedback without pointing fingers in frustration and with the purpose of improving for the next performance, the storm can be beneficial—just as a rainstorm is beneficial to anything that needs water to grow.

Toxic storming is the exact opposite of healthy storming. Using the previous scenario, if a team starts to be over-critical with one another, and it turns into a shouting match between players or between players and coaches, this storm can cause serious damage to team chemistry. Instead of rain dropping to the ground to help plants grow, hail falls from the sky creating damage that could be very difficult to repair.

The following three tips will help you create a healthy storm:

Tip: Listen without judging.

Do you ever find yourself thinking more about what you're going to say next rather than hearing what someone else has to say? When we take this approach, we often miss the message. It's also easy to become defensive when a discussion takes place in the storm stage. When we put up the mental barrier, we miss out on the chance to learn and grow.

Tip: Think before you speak.

Tensions run high during storm discussions. It can be tempting to verbally fire back at someone when they make an accusatory comment. It's common to hear a negative comment and then hear someone say, "Yea, but remember when you did....?" While you may have a strong point, it's important to think about how you can say what you need to say without creating a bigger problem. Sometimes, just taking a few seconds to breathe and think allows you to respond in a way that is beneficial and not harmful.

Tip: Give the benefit of the doubt.

No matter how thin you slice it, there are always two sides to any story. So often, we see only a small portion of a situation. We then mentally connect the dots as to what must have happened in a given situation. This leads to speculation and rumors. For example, let's assume someone is performing poorly and a teammate speculates by saying, "Maybe he's not feeling well." Another person hears that statement and passes it on, but this time they fail to use the word "maybe." By the time the fourth person, in this informal game of "Telephone" hears it, the person has pneumonia! Even if you see a teammate do something that seems out of character or odd, give them the benefit of the doubt. Seek to learn the real story if it's your business and only speak the facts—don't speculate. Following this tip will decrease drama and increase respect.

Every team will face a variety of storms. How we navigate through the storms will affect team chemistry.

Stage 3: Norm The *norm stage* follows the storm stage. Storming can shake things up on a team. Clarity often appears after the storm passes. Think about what it's like after a heavy rainstorm. Usually things are washed clean, plants are green, and  you might even see a rainbow. Teams can have clarification after a storm as teammates have a better understanding of future plans. For example, a player recently joined the team and is now playing in a position that another player normally played in the past. There was probably a storm prior to this move, because it's difficult to surrender a position to a new kid. After people have accepted the new roles, the *new norm* allows people to get accustomed to and comfortable with the new look of the team. After several weeks, most teammates don't remember how it used to be and are more focused on the future instead of dwelling on the past.

Stage 4: Perform When teammates are clear on roles and norms, it's time to perform! The perform stage takes place in practice and in competition. The best teams practice like they want to play. Inconsistent teams believe they can slack off in practice and then turn it up when game time rolls around. This is a quick way to have a disastrous season. When a team practices like they expect to play, there are fewer surprises during a game. For example, if a team goes at half speed for three days prior to a big game, the speed and tempo of the game can throw a team off mentally. As a team leader, it's vital to be a role model of the concept of practicing like you play.

> "Don't lower your expectations to meet your performance. Raise you level of performance to meet your expectations."
> —Ralph Marston

Stage 5: Reform You and your team have practiced hard all week preparing for your crosstown rival. The game plan is in place, and everyone is feeling confident that the team is going to win. Then something goes wrong. A key teammate becomes ill hours before the game and can't participate. Maybe someone gets hurt warming up, or the opponent has anticipated your new game strategy and the surprise strategy doesn't affect them at all. Now what? You have now entered the reform stage of team chemistry. In sports, things can change in a hurry. The teams who can quickly reform will be the most successful.

Reforming might look like adjusting a lineup prior to the start of the game or after a time-out depending on your sport. Many times, the coaching staff will make the changes, but it's up to the team and especially team leaders to trust the coaches and implement the changes. If you look at the Stages of Team Chemistry chart, Reform is on the outside of the chart. It's on the outside because individuals and teams must reform constantly during practice, competition, and the season. It's very possible the people who were seeing a lot of playing time at the beginning of the season are not playing as much at the end of the season because some individuals vastly improved during the season. Depending on the sport and opponent, there may be situations where some players fit the game plan better one week and not the next.

For teams that have individuals who are more interested in individual goals than team goals, the reform stage spells trouble. The inflexible nature that "me first" individuals project can outweigh efforts to reform quickly. However, if the team chemistry is strong and relationships have been forged prior to and during the season, the team welcomes the reform stage. Whatever challenging situation is thrown the team's way, they embrace it and forge ahead.

I had a conversation with a young man who was a star football receiver and played four years of college ball. He played on a college team that threw the ball to several receivers. Grant went from a player accustomed to catching 15 passes to catching three. I asked him how he reformed and adapted to this change. He said, "The receivers made a decision that if the opponent has to focus on covering every receiver instead of one, the team will be more successful. We were genuinely happy when another guy caught the ball because it showed our commitment to the team first." During Grant's senior year in college, they won their division and went deep into the playoffs. His story is a great example of how strong team chemistry can pay off in a season of significance.

> We were genuinely happy when another guy caught the ball because it showed our commitment to the team first.

Teamwork makes the dream work!

One might think there is somewhat of a hierarchy with all five stages and that one stage is less valuable than another. Ideally, a team will progress quickly to the performing stage and stay there all season. As we know, things rarely go perfectly in sports or life. A team that has experienced all five stages is qualified to work through them in pursuing a season of significance.

In his book *The Winner Within*, Pat Riley hits the nail on the head when he describes teamwork. He says, "My driving belief is this: great teamwork is the only way to reach our ultimate moments, to create breakthroughs that define our careers, to fulfill our lives with a sense of lasting significance."

He then says, "Our best efforts, combined with those of our teammates, grow into something far greater and far more satisfying than anything we could have achieved on our own. Teams make us part of something that matters. They are the fountain from which all our rewards will ultimately flow."

Please go to the **Certification Packet** in section three to complete the application exercises for this chapter.

CHAPTER 5

TAKING THE
T.E.A.M. DYNAMICS
PERSONALITY
AWARENESS PROFILE

"The quality of our lives will be determined by the quality of our communication." — Anthony Robbins

Have you ever wondered why you connect with some people easily but may have a difficult time communicating with others? You have probably worked on a classroom project or participated in a sport where everything seemed to just flow. Even though there were many different personality types in the group, everyone seemed to understand their role and the results were outstanding.

And, you've probably known a teacher or coach who seemed to know exactly how to communicate with and motivate different types of people. Maybe they were humorous and upbeat with one person and gave a serious, very detailed plan to someone else. In each instance, however, their method or approach connected and the desired results were attained.

With a better understanding of leadership styles—your own and others'— you can learn the skills and strategies to connect, communicate, and motivate others effectively. Several years ago a learning company in Rochester, Minnesota called Peer Power, and my company, Winning Edge Seminars, created a leadership indicator designed to improve a team's connection and communication. Thousands of students, athletes, educators, and other professionals worldwide have found incredible insight by completing the survey. It's called the "T.E.A.M. Dynamics Leadership Indicator. The indicator that blends individual roles into team goals."

The next several chapters take a deep dive into understanding leadership roles. You'll start this learning process by taking the *T.E.A.M. Dynamics Leadership Indicator*. This exercise will reveal your dominant and supporting leadership styles. You will also:

- Learn about four leadership styles.

- Understand your leadership style in more depth.

- Develop a new appreciation of other people's leadership styles.

- Learn specific strategies to connect and communicate with others.

- Navigate conflict with others whose style of leadership differs from yours.

- Recognize each style has natural strengths, challenges, and room for improvement.

When I present this survey in a live workshop, there are countless "aha!" moments among participants. Students often say after the program they have finally figured out why they have such a difficult time with certain people and more importantly, what they can do about it. This insight can be a game-changer for leaders. Let's get started.

Instructions

You will need a writing utensil for this exercise.

As you look at the survey on the next page, you will see twelve sets of descriptive words or phrases.

For each set, choose the word or phrase that is most like you. For best results, do not spend a lot of time on each answer—go with your first instinct. Once you decide on the word or phrase that is most like you, write a 4 next to it.

> A **3** True to your word
>
> B **1** Innovator
>
> C **4** Thinks things through
>
> D **2** Energetic

There will be three remaining words or phrases that do not have a number next to them. Of the remaining three words or phrases, which one describes you the most? Place a 3 next to that word or phrase. Of the two remaining words or phrases, place a 1 in the box next to the word or phrase that least describes you. Finally, write a 2 on the final empty line.

Each set of four words or phrases requires using all four numbers.

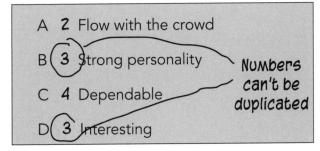

> A **2** Flow with the crowd
>
> B (**3** Strong personality
>
> C **4** Dependable
>
> D (**3** Interesting

Numbers can't be duplicated

At times it may be difficult to determine which word or phrase is most like you, because two characteristics may be very similar. If you encounter this situation, do your best to determine which one slightly outweighs the other.

Remember!

➡ There is no right or wrong answer

➡ A 4 represents the word or phrase that is most like you.

➡ A 1 represents the word or phrase that is least like you.

➡ A number can't be used twice within a set of four words/phrases. Please use a 1,2,3, and 4 for each to ensure clear results.

T.E.A.M. Profile

Directions: Place the appropriate number next to each descriptive phrase.

1   2   3   4

Least   Most

Sample

A	3
B	1
C	4
D	2

A _____ True to your word
B _____ Innovator
C _____ Thinks things through
D _____ Energetic

A _____ Understanding
B _____ Takes charge
C _____ Accurate
D _____ Achiever

A _____ Thoughtful of others
B _____ Daring
C _____ Wants all information
D _____ Laughs easily/Witty

A _____ Giving
B _____ Does own thing
C _____ Cautious
D _____ Articulate

A _____ Will do as instructed
B _____ Risk taker
C _____ Wants things to be exact
D _____ Persuasive

A _____ Humble
B _____ Refuses to give up
C _____ Likes routine
D _____ Leads the pack

A _____ Listens and remains calm
B _____ Winning is very important
C _____ Deliberate
D _____ Enthusiastic

A _____ Flows with the crowd
B _____ Strong personality
C _____ Dependable
D _____ Interesting

A _____ Hides feelings
B _____ Courageous
C _____ Has high standards
D _____ Likes to talk

A _____ Does not rock the boat
B _____ Speaks openly & boldly
C _____ Plays by the rules
D _____ Gets others involved

A _____ Friendly to others
B _____ Decisive
C _____ Wants order
D _____ Outgoing

A _____ Wants others involved
B _____ Results driven
C _____ Difficult time deciding
D _____ Optimistic

Add up totals for each letter and record in the appropriate box below

TOTALS: A= [   ]   B= [   ]   C= [   ]   D= [   ]

© Peer Power—Duplication is illegal.

PERSONALITY AWARENESS PROFILE GRAPH

Directions: *With a dot, mark your (A) total on the Togetherness line,*
(B) total on the Enterprise line, (C) total on the Analyzer line, and
the (D) total on the Motivator line.

TOGETHERNESS **(A TOTAL)**	**E**NTERPRISER **(B TOTAL)**	**A**NALYZER **(C TOTAL)**	**M**OTIVATOR **(D TOTAL)**

My Leading Role   My Support Role   My Villian Role

© Peer Power—Duplication is illegal.

Scoring Your Results To score your survey, add up the values next to each word or phrase. For example, assume you wrote a 3 next to the "A" response in the first set of words and phrases, "True to your word." Then, in the next set of words or phrases, you wrote a 2 next to the "A" response, "Thoughtful of others." The subtotal for the "A" response is now 5. After you have added the values of all "A" responses, write that number in the "A" box at the bottom of the profile next to the word "TOTALS."

Add up totals for each letter and record in the appropriate box below:

TOTALS: A = 40   B = 28   C = 31   D = 21

Repeat the process with the B responses, C responses, and D responses. To ensure the addition is accurate, simply add up all four of the total boxes. If your math is correct, the four boxes should total up to 120. If you don't arrive at 120, go back through your addition to find and fix the error.

Graphing your results The next step is to graph your results on the grid page. Using a dot, mark your A total on the Togetherness line, B total on the Enterpriser line, C total on the Analyzer line, and the D total on the Motivator line. Starting at the dot on the Togetherness line, draw a line to the dot on the Enterpriser line. From the Enterpriser dot, draw a line to the Analyzer line. Finally, draw a line from the Analyzer dot to the Motivator dot.

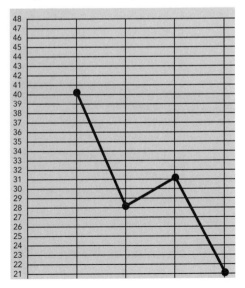

Your Leading Role, Supporting role, and Villain Role

The next step in this exercise is to determine your leading, supporting, and villain roles. The *leading role* is your dominate role, represented by the highest dot on your chart. The supporting role is your next highest dot, and the villain role is your lowest dot.

Determine your Leading Role

Your leading role is your dominant role. Locate it by finding the "peak" (highest) dot on the grid. For example, if the highest dot is on the Togetherness line, your leading role is Togetherness.

Write the leadership style of your leading role on the line provided. In the example (right), Togetherness would be the leading role.

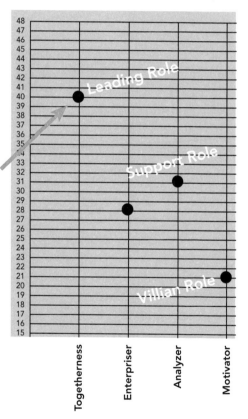

Leading Role: _____

If you have a tie for the leading role, write both leadership styles on the line.

Determine your Supporting Role

Your supporting role can also be considered your *complementary role*. The dot that is second highest from the peak is your supporting role. In a pressure or stressful situation, it is common for people to bring forward their supporting role. Write your supporting role on the line provided.

If you had a tie for leading roles, you can leave the supporting role line blank. If you have a tie for supporting roles and NOT a tie for leading roles, write both supporting roles on the line below.

Supporting Role: _____

Determine your Villain Role

The villain role is the style that is least like you. Find the dot that is the lowest point on the grid. Write that style on the line below. If there is a tie, write in both styles. You will probably find a person with this style is the most difficult for you to communicate with and be around. Basically, the villain role is the opposite of your style.

Villain Role: _____

What's Your Next Move?

Now that you have identified your leadership style, in the next several chapters we will look at each leadership role individually, including its strengths, challenges, and how it can work with and adjust to the characteristics of the other leadership styles.

To help you remember each leadership style, a "scope" has been assigned to each one—stethoscope, microscope, telescope, and kaleidoscope. These associations will become a visual reference for you to remember as you interact with others.

All four leadership styles have advantages and disadvantages. Furthermore, each style might require you to make adjustments when interacting with teammates who have a different style. Being aware of these factors is important when taking on a leadership role. It's important to understand that there is no "correct" style for a team leader. Each style adds something different and important to a team.

> It's vital to honor differences in leadership style. To do so, you need to understand the characteristics of the other leadership styles.

The next several chapters describe each leadership style in detail, including:

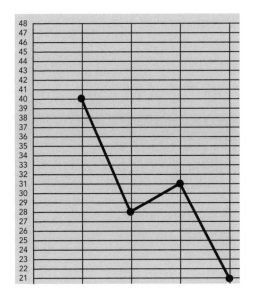 Common characteristics

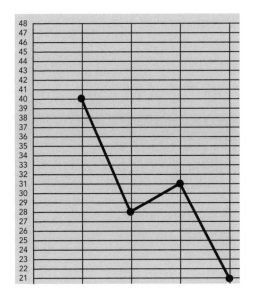 Communication process

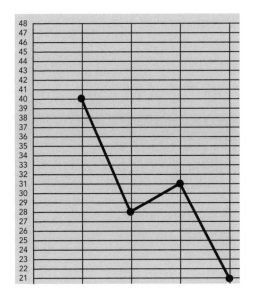 Motivating factors

 Demotivating factors

 Challenges

 Managing relationships with other styles

 Areas for improvement

As you read the description of each style, keep in mind the greater the difference between the points on the grid, the more accurate each description becomes.

In other words, if the difference between a person's dominant role and his/her villain role is only a few points, reading the description of the dominant role may be a true indicator of how the person leads. The leader who has a line graph that curves gently, however, may read all the descriptions and see a part of him/herself in each style.

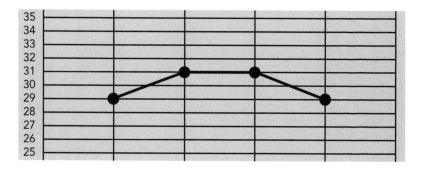

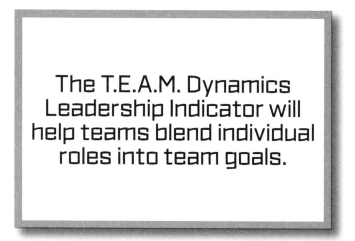

The T.E.A.M. Dynamics Leadership Indicator will help teams blend individual roles into team goals.

CHAPTER 6

UNDERSTANDING THE TOGETHERNESS STYLE

"Wherever you go, go with all your heart." — Confucius

The Togetherness style is represented by the stethoscope. The stethoscope is used to listen to a person's heartbeat or other internal sounds. Leaders with a Togetherness leading role tend to be the heart of the team. They are very aware of other people's feelings and can sense when there is an uneasiness with friends, teammates, and coaches. The higher a person scores on the Togetherness style (the higher the dot is on your chart), the truer the following descriptors will be for you.

Characteristics

- Big hearted
- Consistent
- Reliable
- Loyal
- Keeps others involved
- Strong work ethic
- Wants projects in a step-by-step process
- Takes a lot to make them vent their frustrations

Communication Process

1. Listens and evaluates
2. Decides on a response
3. Responds with sensitivity
4. Reevaluates

Motivating Factors

- Receives positive feedback and appreciation from others
- Appreciates verbal or written recognition
- Lives in a predictable, constant environment
- Provides support or service to others
- Works cooperatively with others
- Rewards quality and accuracy
- Acknowledges feelings

Demotivating Factors

- Managing constant change
- Having to become aggressive with others
- Working all by themselves
- Forced to make a decision immediately
- Dealing with lack of appreciation
- Handling broken promises
- Being publicly embarrassed
- Forced to think only objectively and not consider other people's feelings

Challenges

- Making decisions
- Standing up for feelings
- Facing unclear directions or vision
- Saying "no" when others ask for help
- Voicing their opinion after being rejected

Conflict Management Tendencies

- May give in to avoid looking bad or losing approval
- Tends to avoid interpersonal aggression
- Works as a peacekeeper with others
- Withdraws to plan response
- Becomes rigid
- May withdraw physically
- Becomes emotional

Areas for Improvement

- Increase flexibility; go with the flow
- Ask clarifying questions
- Share ideas after initial rejection
- Vent frustrations

Togetherness Approach to Leading a Team

Togetherness leaders tend to lead more by example than being a vocal leader. Because they may not be vocal, they may not be perceived as a strong leader. Togetherness leaders are strong leaders; they are just not as vocal as other styles. At times, getting everyone's opinion and trying to make everyone happy will stress out the Togetherness leader. Togetherness leaders become more effective when they use their ability to involve others, listen to ideas, and then take action. When Togetherness leaders understand it's impossible to have 100% approval on all ideas, they have a mental breakthrough. Togetherness leaders are a real asset to a team, because their work ethic and ability to relate and understand others is incredibly strong.

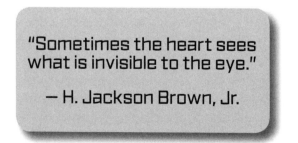

"Sometimes the heart sees what is invisible to the eye."

— H. Jackson Brown, Jr.

Advantages

People who have a Togetherness leading role are very good about including others. It's important for them to

make sure everyone feels involved and valued. In sports, they may go out of their way to connect with all teammates, from the starters to people who seldom play. They are in tune with their team and can sense when there is an unspoken conflict within the group. They are good at mediating a conflict to a solution. The bottom line: They care about the well-being of the team.

Disadvantages

It's not uncommon for the people with the Togetherness style to take things too personally. If someone doesn't like their idea, they can shut down rather than defending their thought or comment. If someone is very direct with a togetherness person, they have a tendency to interpret the way the information is

being delivered rather than the value of the feedback. Sometimes others will hold back giving feedback to a person strong on Togetherness, because they fear the information will be taken too personally and thus reduce the chances of improving a given situation.

Working with Enterprisers

Many Togetherness leaders have a villain role of Enterpriser. Togetherness people tend to be relationship driven, whereas Enterprisers tend to be task driven. It's not uncommon for an Enterpriser to be intimidating to a Togetherness individual. The Enterpriser is considered brash and doesn't understand how their words can be taken to heart. For the Togetherness and Enterpriser to connect, the Togetherness style should make the following general adjustments:

- Don't take their direct behavior personally.
- Listen to their thoughts completely.
- Decide to either share your thoughts or ideas or remain quiet.
- If you remain quiet, do not complain that your ideas are never heard.
- Direct the Enterpriser's vision to stay on task and remind them to take action today for results tomorrow.
- Don't let what *appears* to be anger prevent you from stating your point.

Specific Adjustments for Sports

- Remember that the Enterpriser's loud voice does not always equal anger.
- Avoid believing you know what the Enterpriser is thinking based on his/her facial expressions.
- Speak up.
- Challenge them.
- Calm them down after a mistake.
- Tell them to watch their words if they are making an official angry.

Working with Analyzers

Analyzers have more in common with Togetherness people than Enterprisers do. One characteristic Togetherness and Analyzers share is thinking things through. Both styles would rather take their time to do something right than do something quickly that needs to be done again. "Why do something poorly if your name is going on it?" is a common thought with both styles.

There are also some distinct differences between the two styles. When it comes to group projects, the Togetherness style prefers to work with a group of people instead of working on something alone. The exception is if the group is very brash and doesn't let everyone participate. The Togetherness style also gets upset when they end up doing a majority of the work while others are goofing off. For the Togetherness style to connect with the Analyzer, the Togetherness style should make the following adjustments:

- Think about what you are going to say before you say it.
- Do your part when working with them on a team.
- Give them time to think and ponder the answer to a question.
- Avoid checking in with them too often on the progress of a project. If they said they will complete a task, they will.
- Provide the reason or rationale as to why it's important to do something. Saying "That's just the way it's always been done," doesn't work.
- Use their logic skills to explore options when brainstorming.
- Involve them in organizing.

Specific Adjustments for Sports

- ➡ Notice the little things they are doing.

- ➡ Make suggestions on how they can improve their performance.

- ➡ Ask for their input on how you can improve.

- ➡ Direct them to an article or video on your sport that they might find interesting.

- ➡ Have them "break down" the contest by looking at game film.

- ➡ Ask them to look at game film of an opponent to pick up tendencies (make sure this is within league rules and guidelines).

Working with Motivators

The Togetherness and Motivator styles share the need to develop and nurture relationships. Being around other people is important to the Togetherness style. The exception to this is if others are negative in nature. If that's the case, most Togetherness people would rather be by themselves and search for others who are more positive to be around.

Most Togetherness people enjoy being around Motivators because they provide comic relief in many situations. At times, Togetherness people will plant an idea to say or do something that's a little "out there" to get the Motivator to take action. Motivators will hear that suggestion, see it as a chance to be funny, and will take action on the sketchy idea. There are times when the Motivator will go too far and say or do something that is considered out of bounds by a Togetherness person.

For the Togetherness style to connect with the Motivator, the Togetherness style should make the following adjustments:

- Understand that a majority of what Motivators say is hot air.

- They will most likely promise more than they can deliver.

- They will say some things when trying to be funny that can come across as hurtful.

- Keep them on task, which is difficult for Motivators, because their mind is constantly in motion.

- Use the Motivator's energy to keep the group fired up.

- Check in with them on a regular basis, because they can get off task.

Specific Adjustments for Sports

- Verbally recognize their efforts.

- Challenge them to push themselves.

- Remind them to manage and channel their energy in practice or a contest.

- Keep them focused.

- Hold them back from yelling at an official.

"A good head and a good heart are always a formidable combination."
—Nelson Mandela

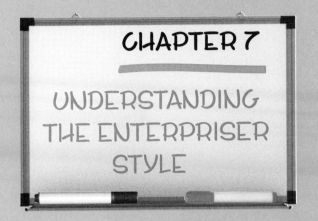

CHAPTER 7

UNDERSTANDING THE ENTERPRISER STYLE

"The only thing worse that being blind is having sight but no vision." — *Helen Keller*

The Enterpriser is represented by the telescope. A telescope helps people see the big picture. It also brings an object that is a long way away into focus. Enterprisers are driven by results. Many times, they would rather get started on something and adjust for success rather than conduct exhaustive research before starting something new.

Characteristics

- Big-picture perspective
- Task oriented
- Action oriented
- Loves to lead
- Hates to lose
- Gets things done
- Hard worker, especially when they care about the project or sport
- Thrives on pressure
- Highly confident

Communication Process

1. Listens selectively
2. Evaluates rapidly
3. Responds quickly
4. Briefly reevaluates

Motivating Factors

- Having control over situations
- Working in a constantly changing environment
- Speaking openly and boldly
- Achieving results based on ends, not means
- Thriving in situations in which creativity can be tapped
- Performing under pressure
- Directing other's actions
- Hearing verbal recognition

Demotivating Factors

- Appearing soft or weak
- Facing situations that require routine, predictable behavior
- Having to outline a task in a step-by-step format
- Dealing with others who take conflict personally
- Being patient when changes take too long
- Starting but not completing projects
- Working with people who withhold feelings or thoughts

Challenges

- Explaining highly detailed ideas and situations
- Getting off track
- Listening all the way through until the end
- Can appear to be insensitive to others
- Can appear to be closed-minded

Conflict Management Tendencies

- Takes a direct, aggressive approach
- Creates win/lose outcomes
- May appear to be mad when simply airing thoughts
- Increases the level of aggression rapidly
- Attempts to clear the air in one meeting

Areas of Improvement

- Get others involved

- Listen to all available options

- Treat others with respect

- Make sure others see the vision

- Stay composed

Enterpriser's Approach to Leading a Team

Enterprisers are usually willing to take on a leadership role. Others may actually perceive them as leaders because they are vocal and creative. Most people enjoy the  Enterpriser's out-of-the-box nature. At times, however, Enterprisers can be viewed as the person who enjoys the spotlight and takes credit for the group's work. The Enterpriser can get to the next level of leadership by honoring others' contributions and involving team members. Their competitive nature, however, can take the team to a whole new level. The key is to get to that level without losing relationships in the process.

Advantages

People who have an Enterpriser leading role are very good at seeing what most people don't. Because of their creative nature, they often devise nontraditional solutions to problems. In situations in which most people would give in or give up, they will find a way to work though the issue. Their competitive nature can bring out the best in other people.

Because they are not really concerned about what other people think, they will say what needs to be said, even if the truth hurts. Their convincing nature attracts others to follow them into unknown territory.

Disadvantages

At times the Enterprisers' strengths become their weaknesses. Because an Enterpriser is quick to think and quick to act, it's common for them to say and do things that they later regret. At times they will be perceived as pushy or brash when communicating. Furthermore, many Enterprisers have a short fuse during conflict. They may

go off on someone and win the argument. Too often, however, when they win the argument, people around them don't appreciate the way the Enterpriser went about winning. Athletes with an Enterpriser leading role must watch their temper in practice and competition. If they are visually angry after an official's call, for example, it could easily come back to hurt them and the team with a technical foul (depending on the sport).

Working with Togetherness

It's very common for Enterprisers to have Togetherness as their villain role. Enterprisers tend to be results driven, whereas the Togetherness style tends to be more relationship driven. Most Enterprisers view the Togetherness leaders as people who want everyone to be happy with group decisions. Enterprisers can get frustrated with Togetherness people because they have to watch their words more carefully instead of just saying what's on their mind. At times, Enterprisers will appear to be mad when, in fact, they are not. They usually want to connect with Togetherness, but if they don't, the Enterpriser is willing to move forward without their support. For the Enterpriser and Togetherness style to connect, Enterprisers should make the following adjustments.

- Ask them their thoughts as they may not immediately jump into a conversation.

- Listen to them completely without interrupting.

- Choose your words wisely.

- Understand that if you become visibly upset with them, they will remember it even if you don't.

- Appreciate their work.

- Know that a pat on the back or a kind word works better than an in-your-face lecture.

Specific Adjustments for Sports

- ➡ Be aware of your tone of voice.

- ➡ Know that what you say is going to be remembered for a long time.

- ➡ Don't promise something if you can't deliver.

- ➡ Recognize their efforts.

- ➡ Avoid getting in their face after a mistake.

- ➡ Avoid putting things off until the last minute.

Working with an Analyzer

It's also common for Enterprisers to have the Analyzer as a villain role. Both styles are motivated by the task and getting the job done. But, Analyzers want things done right whereas Enterprisers want things done now. Another challenge Enterprisers and Analyzers face when working together is the pace of their speech. Most Enterprisers are quick to respond to questions and enjoy throwing out a ton of ideas, whereas Analyzers prefer to filter their thoughts before throwing out ideas that won't work. Enterprisers and Analyzers share the ability to create nontraditional solutions to problems.

For the Enterpriser and Analyzer to connect, Enterprisers should make the following adjustments:

- When asking a question, give them time to think about their response.

- Avoid quickly criticizing their thoughts or ideas.

- Provide a deadline for projects to avoid over thinking.

- Be willing to look for the right solution, not just a quick solution.

- Acknowledge their contributions.

Specific Adjustments for Sports

- Give specific tips and advice on improving performance.

- Avoid getting loud just to prove your point.

- Focus on solutions in a calm fashion.

- Know your opinions are not always right.

- Avoid speaking before you think.

- Understand they may be fired up even though it may not appear that way.

Working with a Motivator

It's common for Enterprisers to have a Motivator as a supporting role. Both styles share a need for energy and creativity. Both styles believe any decision is better than no decision. Many times Enterprisers and Motivators feed off of each other. When the two styles are brainstorming, they can generate several ideas. While a majority of the ideas will not be useable, they believe at least one or two will. When the two styles combine, however, it can turn into a "one up" game. If one style has accomplished something and tells a group about it, the other style may try to "one up" the other's accomplishment. Watching a Motivator and Enterpriser work together is a fun, energetic experience provided they can stay on task and not just throw out ideas. For the Enterpriser and Motivator to connect, Enterprisers should make the following adjustments:

- Attempt to stay on task without distracting discussions.

- Aim for one or two good ideas in a discussion instead of 5 to 10 ideas.

- Avoid taking a negative approach in hopes of inspiring them to do better.

- Build off of their idea, even if it's not your idea.

- Create a plan to make something work instead of just talking about it and taking no action.

Specific Adjustments for Sports

- Remind them to manage their energy.
- Keep them fired up even if you are losing.
- Don't let them question or yell at an official.
- Avoid laughing at them when they are trying to be funny at an inappropriate time.
- Recognize great play as often as you can without going overboard.

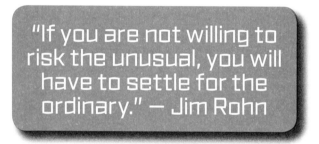

"If you are not willing to risk the unusual, you will have to settle for the ordinary." — Jim Rohn

CHAPTER 8

UNDERSTANDING THE ANALYZER STYLE

"Most people don't plan to fail: they fail to plan."
— John L. Beckley

The Analyzer is represented by the microscope. A microscope has the ability to examine the details of something most people can't see with unaided eyesight alone. The Analyzer can help us diagnose something by taking a closer look. Most Analyzers appreciate clearly communicated expectations and have the ability to solve a puzzle that mystifies many of the other leadership types.

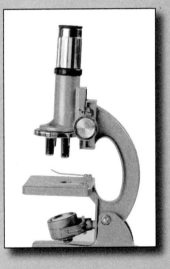

Characteristics

- Thrives on being a big planner
- Approaches situations logically
- Wants all the information
- Thinks things through thoroughly
- Enjoys working independently
- Is always conscious of quality
- Writes their thoughts on paper
- Holds self and others to high standards

Communication Process

1. Listens
2. Evaluates
3. Reevaluates
4. Responds
5. Justifies

Motivating Factors

- Surrounding self with others who will stay on task
- Controlling facts that affect performance
- Taking a logical, systematic approach to tasks
- Solving problems no one else has been able to solve
- Initiating thought-provoking discussions
- Performing to their own standards
- Being right

Demotivating Factors

- Being held responsible to someone else's standards
- Having to make an immediate decision
- Being faced with situations in which a subjective, personal response is required
- Being subjected to rules or expectations that constantly change
- Receiving false recognition
- Having others goof off during crunch times

Challenges

- Accepting others whose standards are different, often considered "lower"
- Making a choice with an adequate amount of information
- Making spur-of-the-moment decisions
- Taking action
- Determining how or why a project or idea won't work

Conflict Management Tendencies

- Remains calm
- Overpowers others with facts and logic
- Requests extensive instructions when faced with new situations
- May withdraw to decide on response strategy
- Resists quietly
- Withholds information
- Becomes defensive. May say, "That's not how it was explained to me."

Areas for Improvement

⇨ Increase flexibility; become comfortable going with the flow

⇨ Find a way to make a project or idea work

⇨ Explain to others why the details are important

⇨ Combine your idea with others' ideas

Analyzers' Approach to Leading a Team

Analyzers can be great leaders. Because they are predictable, they can be relied on to get the job done. It's important for Analyzers to show some enthusiasm, however, when leading a group. While showing emotion and enthusiasm may feel awkward for the Analyzer, the other styles need to see your desire to achieve the best results possible.

After a point has been made, move on to the next point or issue. If Analyzers continue to dwell on the same point over and over, the rest of the styles can lose interest and focus. It's important for Analyzers to use their strengths in organization and logic to help the team or group reach a new level.

Advantages

People characterized as the Analyzer leading role are good at keeping the details together, because they are normally organized in life, they know where things are and what needs to be done. They have the ability to plan an event from a big picture perspective, but also stay focused on a task at hand. Their ability to anticipate potential problems allows them to have back-up plans for anything they are planning. Other styles appreciate the Analyzer's ability to keep emotions under control during a problem, conflict, or crisis. Analyzers also enjoy seeing the plan or idea work to perfection.

Disadvantages

 At times Analyzers will be viewed as not being a high-energy leader. Others can mistake their methodical approach as someone who doesn't have passion for the sport or a particular idea. While it may not appear they are fired up inside, they are excited about being in a leadership role. Because they are detail oriented, Analyzers become frustrated when others don't live up to their commitments or promises. Some styles have a difficult time with the Analyzer's mentality to dot the "i" and cross the "t". Because Analyzers would prefer to make the right choice—instead of just any choice—the delay in verbalizing their decision can be frustrating for others.

It's very common for Analyzers to have a villain role of either Enterpriser or Motivator. Enterpriser and Motivators are usually seen as "big talkers" and "full of themselves" by the Analyzer. Because Enterprisers and Motivators can dominate a conversation, the Analyzer can feel left out despite the fact that they have great ideas that could add to the team. Analyzers hate being cut off in the middle of a conversation because an Enterpriser or Motivator gets an idea of their own and starts to discuss it or says, "That will never work," without even hearing the rationale behind the thought. For these reasons, it can be difficult for Analyzers to work with either style.

Working with Togetherness

Analyzers and Togetherness share the skill of organization. Both styles like to know what's expected of them and don't like last minute surprises or a sudden change of plans. They usually have a strong work ethic, and it frustrates them when other people are goofing off while they are doing the work. It's not uncommon for others to take their work for granted as they seldom seek recognition for what they have accomplished. However, there are some differences in how each style approaches a project or task.

For the Analyzer and Togetherness to connect, Analyzers should make the following adjustments:

- Invite them into conversations if they are being quiet.
- Spend some time talking about personal areas of interest.
- Allow them to work on their own without constantly checking in with them.
- Understand that the tone of your words plays a role in how they perceive the message.
- Appreciate their work verbally.

Specific Adjustments for Sports

- Avoid overloading them with work because they won't say no.
- Understand your words and tone of voice will be remembered.
- Recognize efforts that others seem to miss.
- Provide specific ideas to improve performance.
- Show you care about them.

Working with Enterprisers

Analyzers and Enterprisers are both task driven. Analyzers like to see things done right, whereas Enterprisers like to see action even if the action isn't right. It's common for Analyzers to have a villain role of Enterpriser. Analyzers do not like to be rushed into making a decision, and Enterprisers usually demand it. Analyzers prefer to think about their thoughts before they are spoken; Enterprisers, in turn, seldom filter their thoughts. For these reasons, it can be difficult for the two styles to work together effectively. With some adjustments, however, the Analyzer and Enterpriser can be a powerful combination. For the Analyzer to connect with the Enterpriser, the Analyzer should make the following adjustments:

- ➡ Share your ideas even if you are not "invited" or asked to share.

- ➡ Try to keep the Enterpriser focused on the discussion or task at hand.

- ➡ Understand when they appear to be mad or upset, they are probably just passionate about the idea.

- ➡ When asking specific questions, avoid a sarcastic or doubtful tone.

- ➡ Use your logic skills to make their ideas become a reality.

Specific Adjustments for Sports

- ➡ Don't be intimidated by them.

- ➡ Understand their loud volume doesn't always equal anger.

- ➡ Calm them down after a mistake.

- ➡ Challenge them to get better.

- ➡ Don't let them yell at an official.

Working with a Motivator

It's common for Analyzers to have a Motivator as their villain role. The lack of organization most Motivators exhibit can be frustrating for Analyzers. The random nature of their discussion can also make Analyzers shake their head in disgust. Because Motivators enjoy being the center of attention, they are famous for taking credit for an idea the Analyzer proposed in the first place. Although the two styles approach most situations differently, when they combine their strengths, it's an amazing combination. For example, a Motivator may come up with a creative idea and an Analyzer has the ability to take it from concept to reality.

For the Analyzer to connect with the Motivator, the Analyzer should make the following adjustments:

- Understand Motivators usually speak first and think second.
- Use their creative nature to keep the group fired up.
- Avoid long conversations about all the details.
- Show enthusiasm.
- Use your logic skills to build off of their ideas.

Specific Adjustments for Sports

- Provide specific feedback on improving performance.
- Using an upbeat tone of voice, challenge them to push themselves.
- Remind them to manage their emotions.
- Verbally recognize their efforts.
- Support them after a mistake.
- Give 100% effort.

"Don't just analyze a problem - solve it."
— Kathleen Kennedy

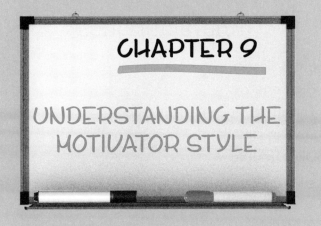

CHAPTER 9

UNDERSTANDING THE MOTIVATOR STYLE

"Find your voice and inspire others to find theirs."
— Stephen Covey

The Motivator is represented by the kaleidoscope. When someone looks into a kaleidoscope everything becomes bigger and brighter. When making a small twist on a kaleidoscope, the view instantly change. Motivators tend to be "go-getters" and enjoy using their creative ability in conversations and projects.

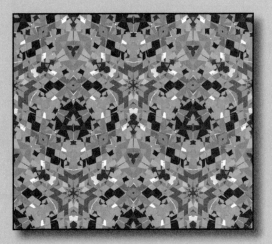

Characteristics

- Enthusiastic
- High energy
- Talkative
- Dislikes details
- Likes people
- Optimistic
- Emotional
- Articulate

Communication Process

1. Listens selectively
2. Responds impulsively
3. Evaluates rapidly
4. Responds again

Motivating Factors

- Positive interaction with others
- Opportunities to verbalize thoughts and feelings
- New challenges
- Rewards for achieving goals
- Frequent change
- Competition
- Inspiring others to achieve results

Demotivating Factors

- Situations where others may react with hostility
- Extensive detail
- Pessimistic surroundings or people
- Repetitive situations that don't change
- Working alone
- Lack of recognition
- People who are always serious

Challenges

- Overuses enthusiasm
- Likes organizing things/events but is just not really organized
- Has several projects going with only a few that are complete
- Actions may not be thought all the way through

Conflict Management Tendencies

- Avoids open, direct conflict
- Attacks others personally
- Seeks revenge by persuading others to take their side
- May seek revenge indirectly
- Becomes emotional
- Minimizes negative information
- Takes criticism or conflict personally
- May openly joke after conflict is over but is still upset

Areas of Improvement

- ➡ Plan things through to the end
- ➡ Concentrate on completion
- ➡ Focus
- ➡ Listen all the way through a conversation
- ➡ Get beyond the idea and take action

Motivator Approach to Leading a Team

Motivators can be great leaders. Because they enjoy being in the spotlight, public speaking is not an issue for them. Motivators get a thrill out of creating a new idea and seeing it become reality. Motivators need to remember to share the spotlight with others. There are a lot of people on the team who work hard for the results. At times, Motivators dominate the conversation and do not seek the ideas of teammates who are quiet or reserved. When they en-

gage the quiet team member, the Motivator will be surprised at how many great ideas are generated. When Motivators not only talk a good game, but walk a good game, the results will be awesome.

Advantages

People who have the Motivator as their leading role normally enjoy being in a leadership role. They enjoy being in front of a group. Because they like talking to whoever will listen, they know a lot of people. Most Motivators enjoy the spotlight of leadership. It's not a problem for them to give their input on a variety of topics. Their sense  of humor and fun nature usually draw others to them. Their high-energy approach to life and sports can help the team excel to a new level.

Disadvantages

Because Motivators enjoy being the center of attention, others can grow frustrated with their antics. Motivators are famous for talking a good game, but sometimes have a difficult time delivering on their promises. As a result, others may not trust that the job will get done. If a Motivator says, "We could do (idea)," others may hear, "Let's do (idea)." To the Motivator, the group was just brainstorming. To others, it's an unfulfilled promise. At times, Motivators will take a situation or joke too far. While Motivators may think they are being funny, others think they have heard or seen enough.

Working with Togetherness

Motivators and Togetherness are both relationship driven. Both styles enjoy being around people and value friendships. Both styles want what's best for the group, but the Motivator can be more vocal with his or her ideas. It's not uncommon for Motivators to dominate a conversation with a Togetherness style. Motivators are famous for talking about what's on their mind instead of engaging the Togetherness style to talk about their life or ideas. As long as the Motivator delivers on promises made, the Togetherness style enjoys the upbeat nature of the Motivator. For the Motivator and Togetherness style to connect, the Motivator should make the following adjustments:

- Invite them into the conversation.
- Recognize their hard work.
- Know a pat on the back will work better than a lecture.
- Trust that if they promise something, they will deliver.
- Know when the joke has gone far enough and recognize when to stop.

Specific Adjustments for Sports

- Be aware of your tone of voice.
- Avoid overloading them with extra work because they have a hard time saying "no."
- Support them after a mistake.
- Make sure they feel a part of the team regardless of their role or playing time.
- Pump them up.
- Recognize their efforts when others don't.

Working with Enterprisers

It's very common for Motivators to have a supporting role of Enterpriser. For this reason, the two styles generally get along and work well together. Many times, Motivators and Enterprisers feed off of each other. When the two styles are brainstorming they can generate several ideas. While a majority of the ideas will not be useable, they believe at least one or two will. When the two styles combine, it can turn into a "one up" game. If one style has accomplished something and tells a group about it, the other style may try to "one up" the other's accomplishment.

One contrast between the two styles is that Motivators are relationship driven and Enterprisers are task driven. Motivators want to accomplish a goal and enjoy doing it with a group of people. Enterprisers are motivated to accomplish a goal with or without a group of people. Enterprisers are not afraid to "do their own thing" as individuals, but the Motivators excel with the energy a group provides. Normally, watching a Motivator and Enterpriser work together is a fun, energetic experience, if they can stay on task and not throw out another idea. For the Motivator and Enterpriser style to connect, the Motivator should make the following adjustments:

- Avoid "one upping" each other.
- Understand the Enterpriser may appear to be mad when he or she is simply passionate.
- Don't take their direct comments too personally.
- Stay focused.
- Know there will be a lot of last minute thoughts and adjustments.

Specific Adjustments for Sports

- ▶ Share a commitment to manage your energy.
- ▶ Be direct yet upbeat with your tone of voice.
- ▶ Don't let them yell at an official in anger.
- ▶ If they are angry with a coach or player, insist they calm down before a confrontation.
- ▶ If they have pushed something too far, speak up or it will continue.
- ▶ Know if they temporarily lose their temper they are probably more passionate than angry.

Working with Analyzers

It's very common for Motivators to have an Analyzer as a villain role. Motivators tend to be random and off-task, whereas Analyzers are more task driven and focused. Most Motivators live in the moment and don't worry too much about planning as "things will work out." This approach can drive an Analyzer crazy. While Analyzers are calm in their daily lives, Motivators are loud and love talking to anyone who will listen. Because of these differences, it can be a challenge for these two styles to work together. However, when they respect each others strengths, it can be a dynamic force. For the Motivator to connect with the Analyzer, the Motivator should make the following adjustments.

- Be as specific as possible when giving instructions or directions.
- Avoid pressuring them for a decision with a short time frame.
- Engage them in the conversation when they are quiet.
- Ask them to think about any problems or loopholes in a plan.
- Give them time to think about their response to a question.

Specific Adjustments for Sports

- ▶ Understand they are still fired up even if it doesn't appear that way.
- ▶ Ask for specific ways you can improve.
- ▶ Engage them to look for tendencies in opponents that might be exploited.
- ▶ Recognize their preparation and effort.
- ▶ Avoid getting in their face.
- ▶ Make sure you know what you are talking about before bringing up a problem or situation.

> **"There's always the motivation of wanting to win. Everybody has that. But a champion needs, in his/her attitude, a motivation above and beyond winning."**
> **—Pat Riley**

CHAPTER 10

PUTTING IT ALL TOGETHER

Observe and Adjust

To be a great leader, it's vital to understand different leadership styles. The T.E.A.M. Dynamics Indicator is a powerful tool. However, it is useless unless you take the time to review not only your own style's tendencies, but information on all the styles. Now that you've

delved into the details, let's look at leadership from a broader perspective.

Ideally, everyone should walk around the world with a Togetherness, Enterpriser, Analyzer, or Motivator button so everyone will know exactly how to connect and communicate. Obviously, that won't happen. The question most people have regarding the styles is this: "What should I do if I don't know someone's leadership style?"

You must become a master observer. Watch how people interact with others. Watch how they respond to a question. Observe how organized they are in their daily life. Watch how they act. If you are a strong observer and understand the tendencies of all four styles, you will be able to make an educated guess. At this point, it's important to know what adjustments to make to connect with a person with a particular style. You can find those details in the previous chapters.

Sometimes people say, "I'm not going to change who I am in order to connect or communicate with someone." Think about that statement for a minute. We are constantly adjusting the way we act. Do we act the same at a dance as we do at an important ceremony? It's doubtful. Do you talk the same way to a three-year-old as you do to a supervisor at work? No way.

If leaders are not willing to change and adjust to the situation and people involved in the situation or group they will be ineffective leaders.

All Styles Create Strength

It's important to remember all four styles are important on a team. Let's use a four-legged chair for this example. Each leg of the chair represents a different leadership style.

If a person wants to stand on a chair with four legs (leadership styles) represented, could they be reasonably confident they could stand firmly on the chair? (The word "reasonably" was added for the Analyzers!)

The answer is "yes." Why? The four legs create balance. Remember, the differences create the strength! If one leg/leadership style was removed from the chair, could someone stand on it? The answer is "probably." You would have to learn and adjust, but it could be done. It's not the ideal situation, but it would work. If a team or group has three out of the four styles represented, they will do well.

If two of the four legs/styles are removed can the chair or team stand? Maybe, but it's going to be a real challenge. It will take a lot of work, and the group will have to dig deep into their supporting roles to do well.

What if there is only one leg of the chair remaining? Could someone stand on it with confidence? The answer is "unlikely." The lack of other legs/leadership styles creates instability.

The same is true on a team. When the different styles work together for a common mission, the differences make the team stronger.

Too Much the Same?

Too often people make the mistake of believing we would be a great team if everyone had the same leadership style. Let's take a closer look at this thought. Let's assume you have a team-building activity, such as building a tower with miscellaneous materials. You have ten minutes to complete the activity.

If the team consists of only Togetherness people, the first five minutes will probably be spent discussing everyone's ideas. Because no one wants to hurt anyone else's feelings, it becomes difficult to get started, and time soon runs out.

If the team consists of only Enterprisers, look out. There would either be a power struggle because each Enterpriser would want to be in charge or nothing would get done because it's just a "stupid" activity anyway.

If the team consists of only Analyzers, time will be an issue. They will take seven minutes to plan it and the remaining three minutes won't be enough to make it happen. If they had 30 minutes, the Analyzers would probably win, because they could execute their plan.

If the team consists of only Motivators, it will be a funny experience. When the activity starts, most Motivators would look at each other and say, "What are we supposed to do? I wasn't really listening." They will have a great time building it with a lot of laughs. However, the tower may or may not get built depending on how much fun the group is having.

As you can see, the thought of everyone being the same leadership style is normally a recipe for disaster.

Embracing and Empowering

The best leaders understand how to embrace and empower all four leadership styles. When everyone's role and leadership is accepted and embraced, a team has a chance to accomplish a season of significance.

After mastering the information in this book, you will be equipped to become a master communicator with people who have different personalities and leadership styles.

You now understand the different languages people speak. By *understanding and owning* knowledge about different leadership styles you have the ability to communicate in different leadership languages.

Please go to the **Certification Packet** in section three to complete the application exercises for Chapters 5 - 10.

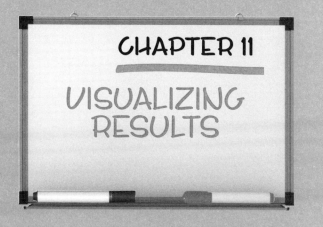

CHAPTER 11

VISUALIZING RESULTS

"I always had something to shoot for each year: to jump one inch further." — Jackie Joyner-Kersee

This chapter intermixes personal and team goals. As you have already read, some sports have a team **and** an individual aspect, whereas some sports are more team oriented. The content applies to both types of sports. As you read the following strategies, feel free to mentally exchange the "team" concept with "you" or "leaders."

Regardless of the type of sport, leaders look to set team goals first, followed by personal goals.

If you don't know where you're headed, you're going to struggle. It's like jumping into a taxicab without a destination in mind. Imagine the cost of the ride if someone said to the cab driver, "Just drive around for awhile, and when I see the right place, I'll tell you." What a costly approach!

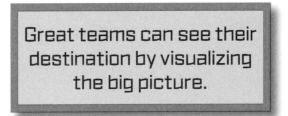

> Great teams can see their destination by visualizing the big picture.

During the grand opening of Disney World in Orlando, Florida, there was a huge celebration. Unfortunately, Walt Disney had passed away prior to the doors opening to the public. After the ceremony, the emcee of the event said to Walt's wife, "It's too bad Walt wasn't here to see it." Mrs. Disney turned to the emcee and said, "Oh, he saw every bit of it in his mind."

Walt Disney and his team saw the big picture. Does your team see the big picture?

If the big picture isn't defined clearly and communicated often, your teammates will begin a chain of complaining. They will complain about physical conditioning, watching films, and the amount of playing time they get. A strong team vision can decrease complaining and bolster team spirit as everyone involved can see the desired result.

To create a strong vision personally and for the team, follow the GOALS formula, which I developed. The GOALS formula has helped thousands of individuals and hundreds of teams reach a desired outcome. Just like exercise equipment, it only works when you use it. While no formula is 100% effective, if you follow the system, you dramatically increase the odds of attaining your goals.

The GOALS formula stands for:

Genuine

Optimistic

Accurate

Listed

Symbols

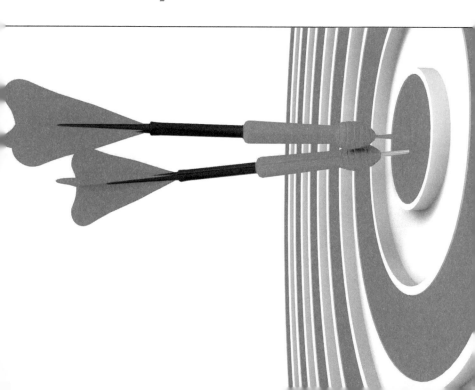

Genuine

Have you ever had someone else set a goal for you? When that happened, were you excited about accomplishing that goal? Usually, the answer is no. You're not pumped about it because it's not your goal. It's not genuine; it's someone else's vision for you.

Genuine looks more like this: Remember when you were a child, and you really wanted a new toy that was being advertised? Unfortunately, you didn't have the money, and your parents said they wouldn't pay for it. What did you do?

Chances are, you got creative and starting earning some money. It's interesting to learn how many opportunities there are to make extra money when you are motivated and want to purchase something. Of course, those same money-making options were there before, but because your desire to earn more money wasn't important, you didn't pay attention to them. Suddenly, when you need additional cash, your mind opens up to all sorts of possibilities.

You may recall the pride and satisfaction of ordering the item online or going to a store to purchase it. Maybe you had a bag full of change and said to a store employee, "I've got just enough." You worked hard because it was your goal—not someone else's.

Optimistic

There are four approaches to setting goals: pessimistic, realistic, idealistic, and optimistic. **Pessimistic goals are for people who expect little from themselves and their team. Realistic goals are for people who expect average results from themselves and others. Idealistic goals are so high in the sky they're impossible to achieve. Optimistic goals are just out of reach, but not out of sight.**

As you define goals for yourself and your team, ask yourself this question: "Is the goal going to be a stretch or will it be simple to reach?" If it's not going to take much effort to accomplish the goal, it won't mean much when you attain it. How do you know if a goal can be considered optimistic? If you're wondering if you can reach that far or work that hard to reach the goal you've set, you're setting optimistic goals.

> If it's not going to take much effort to accomplish the goal, it won't mean much when you attain it. How do you know if a goal can be considered optimistic?
> If you're wondering if you can reach that far or work that hard to reach the goal you've set, you're setting optimistic goals.

Accurate

When I conduct a leader-ship training workshop or a school assembly, I usually start by meeting with a small group of students. This gives me a flavor for school spirit, attitudes, and the overall culture and climate in the building. After visiting for a few

minutes, I ask the students, "What are some of your goals for this school year?" Most look at me like a deer caught in headlights. Typically, I see students shrug their shoulders and sheepishly say, "I don't know, graduate on time, I guess."

Talk about vague, uninspiring goals!

Every once in a while, though, I'll hear, "My goal is to graduate with a 3.5 GPA, be selected all-conference in (my sport), and get accepted into (name of post-secondary school) or (branch of Armed Services).

After a response like that, I smile, and say, "It sounds like you have an accurate view of the future."

Are your goals accurate or vague?

You'll have a greater chance of attaining your goals if they are precise. For example, a hockey team may set a goal regarding the average number of shots on goal, whereas a softball team may set a goal regarding total runs batted in.

If you can communicate the goal with someone you don't know, and they can clearly understand it, you have established an accurate goal.

Listed

Have you ever invited a group of friends for a sleepover? Suddenly it's 3:00 AM and although you've eaten one pizza after another, everyone's still hungry. So, you tiptoe into the kitchen, careful not to wake any family members, and you find a cake mix.

Everyone agrees: It's cake time! You empty the box and start adding the ingredients required. Someone gets the smart idea to just add water and see what happens. Because you're all starving, you crank the temperature to 550 degrees and put the cake mix in the oven. After fifteen minutes, you discover the cake has exploded all over the inside of the oven. What happened?

You didn't follow the recipe.

A recipe is a list of ingredients and the sequence for adding them in order to get the results you desire. If you're going to reach your optimistic goal, you must create a list that shows how you're going to achieve your goal. If your goal is to serve three aces per volleyball match, create a list of what you need to do to improve your serve. The list must be accurate and measurable. If you simply write, "Try harder or practice more," you've created a vague list. However, if you created a list that included items like the following, you're on your way:

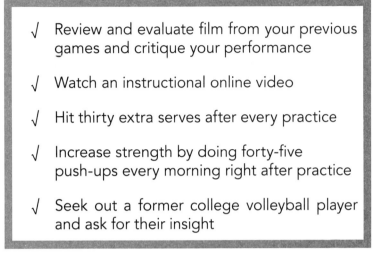

√ Review and evaluate film from your previous games and critique your performance

√ Watch an instructional online video

√ Hit thirty extra serves after every practice

√ Increase strength by doing forty-five push-ups every morning right after practice

√ Seek out a former college volleyball player and ask for their insight

Specific actions will lead you to your goal. Great recipes, just like great goals, have a list that outlines precisely how they will be attained.

"No matter how many goals you have achieved, you must set your sights on a higher one."
— Jessica Savitch

Symbols

Your mind is powerful. Just think about what it does. Have you ever had a dream in which you were falling, and you woke up to find your heart racing? Have you been swimming in a lake and had scary music from a movie thriller start to play in your head that causes you to scramble out of the water? Have you ever heard a song and immediately remembered a person or situation? Have you ever forgotten to set an alarm on your phone, but woke up at the right time anyway?

If you have experienced any of these situations, you've glimpsed the power of your mind. Great teams understand the power of the mind and then harness it to help them reach their goals.

Seeing symbols puts your mind to work. Symbols create a sense of confidence in the mind that says, "This is going to happen." When people see symbols, they start to believe that goal will become reality. Even if you fall short, at least you had the courage to aim your efforts high.

While teaching this concept at a leadership conference, I asked the students to share their goals with their small group. I then asked volunteers to share their goals with the large group. One young man said his goal was to high jump six foot six. If you are not a high jumper, this is a lofty goal for a high school kid. I asked him, "What's your PR so far?" He said his personal record was six feet two inches. Most people would think improving a mere four inches shouldn't be a big deal. If you have experience with the high jump, you know the goal was very optimistic.

My advice to him included purchasing a special tape that wouldn't take paint off the wall when removed. "The brighter color the tape, the better," I instructed. Then, I asked him to measure a height of six foot seven from the floor. *Even though his goal was six foot six, I wanted him to aim a little higher.* Once he marked the optimistic height in his room, the next part was to run the tape along all four walls of his bedroom.

The tape became the symbol for the high jump bar. If he saw the tape every day, I was convinced he would attain the goal—provided he implemented the other principles of the GOALS formula.

I returned to his school for a follow-up session in the fall. The smile on his face said it all when he walked up to me and said, "I jumped six foot six at my final meet last year." It took a while for the goose bumps to calm down on my arms. The goose bumps returned when he said, "This year, I'm gonna jump six foot seven."

The GOALS formula works!

Below is an email from a student who attended a leadership workshop.

Mr. Hillier,

My name is Emily and I attended your seminar in PA a few weeks ago. The part of your seminar that made the most sense to me was the part when you made us visualize ourselves reaching farther back than we did the first time. This seemed to "click" in my head, if you know what I mean. I also thought you might be interested to know that I have been using this in each of my soccer games ever since. This really helped me play well and helped me lead our team to win our first soccer state championship on Friday night!

Thanks, Emily D

Please go to the **Certification Packet** in section three to complete the application exercises for this chapter.

"Life takes on meaning when you become motivated, set goals and charge after them in an unstoppable manner."
— Les Brown

CHAPTER 12

REFUSING DRUGS AND ALCOHOL

"Drugs take you farther than you want to go, keep you there longer than you want to stay, and cost you more than you can ever pay." —Chester Brewer, Jr.

Imagine a smooth voice on a television advertisement asking, "Are you looking for a way to destroy your health, lose friends, and slow your team's progress?" Who would say "yes" to this product? No one! Yet every year teen athletes say yes to illegal drugs, performance-enhancing drugs, and alcohol. Before you skip this chapter because another adult is telling you to "Just Say No," read the information and think about how drugs affect your team— even if you are not the one using them.

What If?

A football team in northern Minnesota won a regional final and was set to play for the state championship. After the regional victory, the team had a party where alcohol was served. On their way home, two all-conference linemen were pulled over by the police and cited for minor consumption. Because of their infraction, they became ineligible for the state championship.

The team lost in the finals. If the two linemen had participated, would the team have won the state championship? No one can answer that question for sure, but everyone will remember that question for a long time. Imagine their ten-year reunion when everyone gathers to share old memories. The conversation among the football team will surely discuss what could have been.

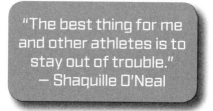

> "The best thing for me and other athletes is to stay out of trouble."
> — Shaquille O'Neal

Now imagine the two former linemen showing up for the reunion and having teammates introduce their significant others by saying, "These are the two guys who cost us the state championship." Do you want to be in that position? It's tempting to say, "Yeah, but..." to this question. "Yeah, but everyone's doing it." "Yeah, but it's tradition." "Yeah, but there's nothing else to do." "Yeah, but I'm not the one taking the drugs—it's them."

These excuses and every other excuse you can imagine just don't cut it. In my work with two million students since 1990, I've heard hundreds of stories of how drugs and alcohol have negatively impacted individuals and teams. I could write an entire book on the stories students have shared with me.

The Effects Are Bigger Than You Think

Often the most popular drug used in schools today is alcohol. Some people tend to think alcohol isn't a drug, because there's a legal drinking age. Cocaine, LSD, heroin, and other drugs are clearly illegal—no matter how old you are. Whether you—or someone on your team—is using alcohol or steroids, they're illegal, even if you purchase them online as in the case of steroids or performance-enhancing drugs.

The detrimental effects of alcohol on performance are well documented and include impairment of the following:

- ▶ Balance and steadiness

- ▶ Reaction time

- ▶ Fine and complex motor skills

- ▶ Information processing

- ▶ Speech

- ▶ Decision making

John Underwood, founder of Athletes for Life, has consulted with high school athletes, college athletes, professional athletes, and even Olympic athletes. He has conducted thousands of performance experiments and has gathered countless brain scans from athletes who have used alcohol and other drugs. I had a chance to see John present slides showing how brain activity suffers with alcohol use. He showed brain slides of slower response time immediately after consuming alcohol, as well as scans from athletes who have used alcohol on a long-term basis. It was riveting to see the detrimental, visible affect alcohol has on our brain. Of course, it also affects our body chemistry and ability to recover and heal after a practice or contest.

The most startling statistic from John's presentation was this:

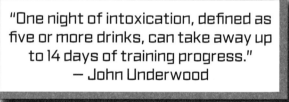

"One night of intoxication, defined as five or more drinks, can take away up to 14 days of training progress."
— John Underwood

Think about that statistic. You work your tail off in the off-season and during the season and one night of intoxication can take away up to 14 days of that hard work!

There are also these long-term results:

- ⮕ Legal problems
- ⮕ Addiction
- ⮕ Being involved in a traffic accident
- ⮕ Engaging in risky, sexual behavior that may spread disease
- ⮕ Decline in general health

How Drugs Affect Your Team

What are the potential side affects of drugs and alcohol on the team? If people are using drugs or alcohol, a downward spiral can begin as they could affect the team's:

- ➔ Spirit

- ➔ Momentum

- ➔ Image

But that's not all. A division between "those using" and "those not using" could destroy a team's sense of unity. Athletes who get caught could be suspended or removed from the team altogether.

So, what do you do if you're a leader, you don't use drugs or alcohol, but you know of team members who do? I think you'd agree that this is a very tough question; there is not a simple answer to this problem. However, it's a question you to need to think about answering. My recommendation is to have a candid conversation with your coach about how to handle this situation. Your goal might be to create a pact with your coach and teammates spelling out what will happen if someone decides to drink alcohol or use illegal drugs.

Remember, being a leader is not a popularity contest. Being drug and alcohol free isn't going to be an easy task given peer pressure these days.

However, by committing to abstain from these dangerous substances, you will certainly have a season to remember, instead of one you wish you could forget.

Take a stand

A wise high school coach of mine once said, "You have the rest of your life to drink if you choose. You only have one chance to participate in high school athletics." I'll never forget that statement. It was right on target, and our football team took it to heart.

On the first day of summer football practice, our coach challenged the team to be drug and alcohol free. He said our team had the potential to have an awesome season. Several of the players on the previous season's team drank a lot of alcohol. Our team knew alcohol played a role in the previous year's poor record and dismal performance.

We were committed to making our senior season different. We were not going to let alcohol wreck our potential.

On that first day of practice, twenty-two seniors and ten juniors pledged to be drug and alcohol free. I'm proud to say that everyone on that team lived up to his word. Our record was 6 and 2, and we went to the playoffs. It was an incredible experience; one I will never forget. Had our team fallen into the tradition of alcohol, I honestly believe we would have had average or less than average results. It certainly would not have been a season of significance.

Even though that was a long time ago, I often reflect on that fall. We were a bunch of young men committing to each other and then playing our hearts out on Friday nights.

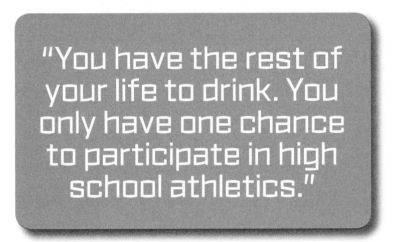

"You have the rest of your life to drink. You only have one chance to participate in high school athletics."

During a pre-season meeting, stand up and present a pledge for teammates not to use drugs and alcohol. If the sport for which you are a leader has a tradition of using drugs and alcohol, this is the year to turn it around. By committing to being drug free, you are eliminating one big thing that could keep your team from doing the best that it can.

Please go to the **Certification Packet** in section three to complete the application exercises for this chapter.

"You don't want to
spend your life
living down
one night
of living it up."

CHAPTER 13

SETTING THE STAGE

"As soon as I accomplish one thing, I just set a high goal. That's how I've gotten to where I am." — Beyonce

You may know the feeling. You're at a live concert featuring your favorite singer or band, and you feel the energy in the arena prior to the start. Suddenly, the house lights shut off and spotlights whip around the room. The background music becomes louder and louder. Finally, after all the excitement and anticipation, the entertainers appear on the stage and the concert begins! A great performance can be etched in your mind for a long time as you relive the incredible experience.

Most people don't realize the daily grind that goes into creating a memorable concert every night. The musical act may have traveled through the night on a tour bus from a previous concert. It takes a large crew at least seven hours to set the stage, lights, screens, and technology. All of the travel, details, preparation, rehearsal, and set up are necessary to produce an extraordinary two-hour concert. And, without all the work behind the scenes, the concert will likely flop. Soon the entertainers discover it's unexpectedly become their final tour, as they are no longer attracting an audience.

Great performers know the value of setting the stage every day!

Team leaders also set the stage for a season of significance. Every time you walk into a team meeting, practice, competition, or are out in the community, you have the opportunity to make a positive impression. Will the stage you set be one that engages others, or will it cause others to lose interest? By committing to each of the Five Keys of setting the stage, you are destined to create an amazing athletic experience.

Be the message

John Crudele, author and speaker, once made a powerful statement. "Your walk talks, and your talk talks, but your walk talks louder than your talk talks." It's also been said, "Who you are speaks so loudly, I can barely hear what you are saying."

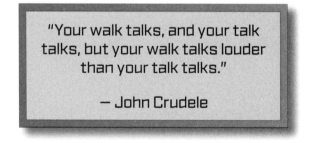

"Your walk talks, and your talk talks, but your walk talks louder than your talk talks."

— John Crudele

Leaders understand they cannot ask someone else to do or be something they are not demonstrating themselves. Imagine the laziest person you know telling people to get off the couch and make something happen and then retreating back to their couch. People would have to pick themselves off the floor from laughing so hard.

Everyone around you evaluates your leadership ability more on the actions they see versus the words you use. Unfortunately, too often the mouth is saying one thing and actions are demonstrating something else.

As a freshman, I was one of a handful of athletes to make the varsity track team. The senior class had some amazing athletes and leaders. One of the very talented athletes wanted to be considered a leader, but his work ethic was weak. With his raw talent, he usually won his events each track meet. But, if he could figure out a shortcut, he took it. His goal was to give no more than 50% effort in practice. And yet, in front of coaches, he was always yelling at everyone to push themselves. It was clear to everyone on the team he was more concerned about looking good than being good.

Prior to the first meet, the entire team was training to build stamina with long distance runs. One day, our coach split us into two random teams and instructed us to run as a pack to two different landmarks and then run back to the track. I was on the squad with the lazy, arrogant leader. This was the first time I was on a varsity team, which made me very nervous. My approach, therefore, was to work hard and keep my mouth shut. *This approach works very well for freshman and sophomores who are asked to be on a varsity team. Acting like you are "all that" is the quickest way to tick off the upperclassmen.*

Strong athletic talent ≠ strong leadership

When we got halfway to our landmark, Mr. Arrogant stopped the squad and said, "This is ridiculous to run this far. Let's just hang out here for 15 minutes and run back. Coach will never know." A few of the older guys hesitantly agreed and the younger ones, including me, didn't say a word. After 15 minutes, we ran back to the track.

What we didn't know was the coach took a different route and was waiting for us at the landmark. He was visibly agitated and especially furious with the senior leaders. The next two days of practice were absolutely brutal for our half of the team. My legs hurt every time I tell the story.

There are no short cuts to any place worth going.

The other half of our split squad ran to their landmark to meet an assistant coach waiting for them as well. Apparently, the senior leaders didn't even consider taking a short cut, as they understood improving stamina would be beneficial for the rest of the season.

Although the experience was painful and embarrassing to learn, two lessons have stuck with me. First, leaders don't take short cuts or put in a halfhearted effort in practice or in a game. Second, leaders' actions can influence the team positively or negatively.

Whether it's your teammates, coaches, or the people in the stands, everyone is watching you. And they watch you even closer when difficult situations arise. If the official makes a bad call, do you lose your composure, stomp your feet, roll your eyes, and let out a huge sigh for everyone to hear? Do you yell at the official? If you do, how can you get upset when a teammate does the same thing?

> You are the example!
> You cannot get what
> you're not willing to give.
> Make sure your walk
> matches your talk.

Show Up Every Day

Showing up is not about attendance. Showing up is about being tuned in and focused on the task at hand. It's easy to let your thoughts drift. When that happens, important instructions or advice can be missed. It's vital to be both physically and mentally present.

Average athletes and teams believe they can mentally show up for just the important contests. Rarely does that work consistently. Sure, some have pulled it off by getting totally focused at the end of the season around tournament time. Attempting to show up only for the important matches usually backfires as old habits creep in and destroy an individual's or team's progress. Leaders who show up every day create a strong habit that will carry them throughout the season and throughout their lives.

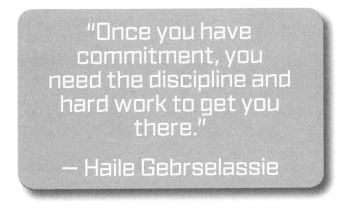

"Once you have commitment, you need the discipline and hard work to get you there."

— Haile Gebrselassie

Jill Esplin, a speaking colleague, shared a powerful experience. Jill played varsity doubles tennis in high school. During her junior year, her tennis partner was going through a rough time due to a breakup with her boyfriend. This situation created outside drama that unfortunately spilled onto the court and affected her performance.

The duo found themselves losing matches that they should have won. The season ended on a low note, and their future as doubles partners was in jeopardy.

Prior to their senior year, Jill and her tennis partner had a crucial conversation about the previous year. They created an analogy to deal with future drama that ended up having an amazing impact for their season. Whenever either player was experiencing difficulty outside the sport, each committed to placing the drama or situation into an imaginary drawer. The drawer would be mentally shut, allowing the tennis partners to focus 100% during practice and matches. Using this mental strategy doesn't imply the difficult situation is to be ignored or minimized. Keep in mind that it's still in the drawer and will be waiting for you when the competition is complete. It does mean, however, that you are willing to honor your sport by dealing with the issue at an appropriate time. Rarely is the appropriate time while practicing or in a game.

Using this strategy, the duo didn't win a state championship, but they improved immensely from their junior year.

There will be rough times for team leaders as well. It's easy to let outside difficulties or distractions affect what

happens inside your sport. When you are willing to mentally put distractions in a drawer—at least temporarily—you can focus in practice or competition. Team leaders owe it to themselves and others to be peak performers. This happens by showing up every day regardless of outside challenges.

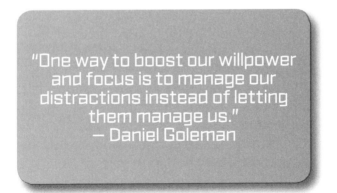

"One way to boost our willpower and focus is to manage our distractions instead of letting them manage us."
— Daniel Goleman

Appreciate Everyone's Role

Not everyone on the team is going to be a star. Some people may be on the team because it's the only positive thing in their life.

One of my best friends in high school averaged eight points a season in basketball. He lived for warm-ups prior to the game. While he wasn't talented on the floor, his sense of humor carried the team a long way. He was quick with a joke and could make anyone smile regardless of the situation. He was the spark plug of the team despite the fact he didn't play very much. His role was to provide comic relief.

As a leader, it's vital to support players at all levels. Remember: athletes develop at different rates. A lanky junior can turn into a whole new player as a senior. If you demean ability, you are driving a wedge between you and your teammates. If you're going to play beyond the scoreboard, respect each person's role on the team. Whether they bring out the water or earn the highest score on the beam, respect everyone's role.

During a live leadership workshop in Michigan, I asked the student athletes to discuss a difficult situation they faced in the past. Students were asked to talk about the event in their small groups along with what could have been better. A junior shared her experience of moving up from the junior varsity to varsity as a sophomore. Although she was excited about the opportunity, two seniors were not thrilled about the situation. During warm-up passing drills, one of the ticked off seniors was throwing the ball as hard as she could at the sophomore's face. As this athlete relived the experience, her voice became shaky. The room went silent when she ended her story with, "I just wanted to help the team. I didn't want anyone hating me for it."

There will be times when your coach makes changes that could involve younger players seeing more playing time. You will have a choice to make them feel "a part of" or "apart from" the team.

You may be in a sport that is both an individual sport with a team aspect such as track, gymnastics, cross-country, wrestling, and so on. If that's the case, creating an atmosphere where underclassmen are welcomed is absolutely vital for the team to perform at its best. In track, for example, the freshman who runs the 1600 meter race at a blistering pace may be the difference between advancing to post-season competition or ending the season prematurely.

> When everyone on the team, freshman to senior, feels his or her contribution matters, you are destined for a season of significance.

Be Up when Others Are Down

Have you ever been on a team when everything starts out wonderful? People get along, the team has a strong winning record, and everyone is healthy? If you have been a part of a team like that, it's easy to be upbeat and positive. It takes no effort at all during such times.

What happens when the opposite occurs? You lose nearly every contest, people are mad because they are not getting enough playing time, and a team star has an injury. Now what? This is the time for a team leader to step up. The team needs you the most at this time.

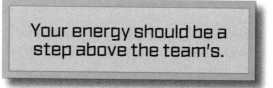

Your energy should be a step above the team's.

Imagine a staircase in front of you that represent energy level. The top stair represents the highest energy and enthusiasm a team could have. The bottom stair represents the lowest level of energy possible.

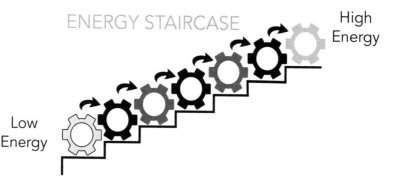

ENERGY STAIRCASE

High Energy

Low Energy

Wise leaders are constantly gauging their team's energy level so they can adjust their personal energy to fit the situation. For example, imagine a team has encountered a rough spot in the season as they lost three contests in a row to teams they were expected to beat. As the team enters practice, the team leaders gauge the team's energy at stair five. While stair five isn't terrible, it isn't great either. A strong team leader understands stair five won't be enough to break through the rut. It may be tempting for the team leader to take his or her personal energy to stair ten in hopes that everyone will do the same. A radical jump from stair five to ten is usually way too much. Maybe you have experienced being at stair five and had someone who is at stair ten try to motivate you. If this has happened to you, it's common to think, "They are way too much for me to handle right now." Instead of that person being motivating, you find them incredibly annoying. Trying to have someone "leap" from stair five to ten in a short time usually backfires.

Great leaders have a strong sense of the team's energy and intentionally start at the same level—at least initially. After a short time, the leader then takes a mental step above the team's energy. In most cases, if the leader has credibility and influence, the team matches his or her energy. It's similar to eating dinner with someone who eats quickly and you suddenly feel the urge to eat faster than your normal eating speed. Or if you have ever been to the Caribbean, you will notice a slower pace of life. The same concept—in reverse—can happen in sports.

Once the team takes a step, a leader takes another step up. The goal is to keep stepping up until the right energy is attained. Keep in mind there is a constant movement up and down the energy stairway. It would be unattainable and unhealthy to be at the top stair every day of your life. Seasoned leaders take the team's pulse and then determine the appropriate path on the energy staircase.

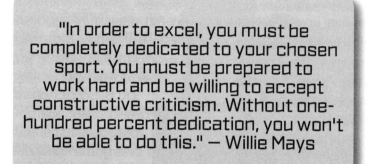

"In order to excel, you must be completely dedicated to your chosen sport. You must be prepared to work hard and be willing to accept constructive criticism. Without one-hundred percent dedication, you won't be able to do this." — Willie Mays

You represent your team all the time

If a complete stranger compliments you on a recent game or performance you may have thought to yourself, "Who was that?"

I was once at a restaurant where a lacrosse team was seated at a large table. For the most part, they were just being teenagers. They were laughing, eating, and having a good time. Toward the end of the meal, they started trashing some players and their head coach who were not in attendance. Their language was raw, complete with every cuss word in the book. Because I was seated right next to them, I could hear every word. Be-

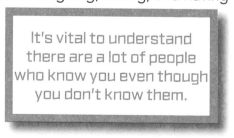

It's vital to understand there are a lot of people who know you even though you don't know them.

cause the restaurant wasn't in my hometown, there wasn't a lot damage done, because I didn't know who they were talking about. But what if I was a friend of the coach or a parent of one of the kids they were criticizing? The lack of awareness could have created a huge team chemistry problem had their conversation been passed along to the coach or the players they were disrespecting.

Conversely, I was bowling one night with my family when a girl's volleyball team was assigned four lanes next to us. The coach decided bowling would provide a break from the day-to-day grind and provide a chance for the team to connect with each other. They were very upbeat, talkative, high school students. Because of my work with athletes, I started asking questions. It was fun to hear about their season and see them interact in a positive way with each other. Before we left, I walked up to the coach and complimented her on how impressive it was to see how the team interacted with each other. Similar to the

previous story, the coach and kids didn't have any idea who I was or who I knew. She simply said, "These girls are awesome—on and off the court."

As a leader, it's imperative to understand there are a lot of eyes on you. While this could be viewed as a burden, great team leaders see it as a benefit.

Great concerts, just like great sports seasons, set the stage for unforgettable memories. By applying the strategies in this chapter, you will no doubt create an abundance of such memories.

Please go to the **Certification Packet** in section three to complete the application exercises for this chapter.

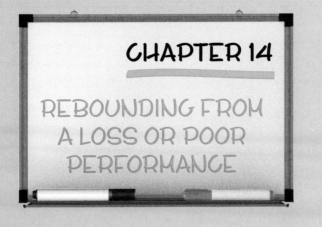

CHAPTER 14

REBOUNDING FROM A LOSS OR POOR PERFORMANCE

"We never let winning go to our head or losing go to our heart." — *Phil Jackson*

After a loss, it's natural to be angry and disappointed, and it's all right to hold on to those feelings for a short time. Such feelings may even serve as motivation to work harder in practice for the next game. Unfortunately, however, many individuals and teams hold on to the loss way too long.

I had the opportunity to interview Karl Mecklenburg, who was an all-American and former professional football player for the Denver Broncos. He started in three Super Bowls. Unfortunately, none of the teams for which he played were able to take home the championship ring. The focus of the interview was rebounding from a loss. The insight from the interview was very useful and practical.

Mecklenburg shared five policies for rebounding from a loss. A policy is a standard or predictable way an individual or a team handles various situations. The best policies are communicated and executed consistently. When everyone adheres to a policy, a team will thrive. If policies are broken, or misunderstood, a team can struggle.

Policies for rebounding from a loss

1. Review and evaluate your performance

2. Understand you will make mistakes

3. Understand others will make mistakes

4. Determine what you can fix

5. Look to improve

> "First, accept sadness. Realize that without losing, winning isn't so great." — Alyssa Milano

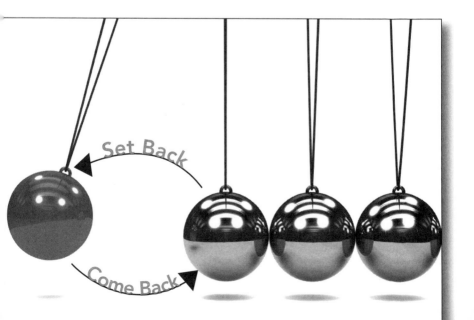

Policy # 1 Review and evaluate your performance

It's important to take the time to mentally review your performance. Without being overly critical, ask yourself:

- "What did I do right?"

- "Where did I mess up?"

- "How prepared was I mentally and physically?"

After you complete the mental review, the next step in evaluating your performance is to watch the game film. This can be very humbling! We tend to think we know how we look when we are involved in our sport. Often, however, seeing on film how we played or performed is a surprise. Yet, the film doesn't lie. By seeing ourselves on film, we gain a new perspective on what we did right and wrong. Taking it a step further, it's valuable to review our performance in slow motion. This approach allows us to isolate things that were done correctly or incorrectly. Despite the uncomfortable feeling of watching our performance in replay, this visual tool can quickly help diagnose the good, bad, and ugly part of our performance. It also provides the ability to track our progress from one contest to the next.

Policy # 2 Understand you will make mistakes

No one is perfect! Regardless of the sport, even the top players make mistakes. Golfers hit the ball in the water; swimmers pace themselves poorly; soccer goalies let an easy goal hit the net. Even a baseball or softball pitcher who had a perfect game threw some pitches that were not strikes. While every athlete strives for a perfect performance, it's rarely going to happen.

> While every athlete strives for a perfect performance, it's rarely going to happen.

Bill Cordes, my friend and colleague, shares a powerful point during live workshops that can be a life changer. He proclaims that, "Mistakes are great moments!" When you make a mistake in life or in sports, saying to yourself, "That was a great moment!" removes some of your internal pressure to be perfect. Adopting this approach is similar to rebooting or restarting a computer that is displaying an error on the screen. The restart normally resets the computer's internal memory, clears the issue or error, and allows you to go back to where you were on the computer. Try this approach the next time you mess up and notice how it works. The quicker you can reset and forgive yourself for a mistake, the faster you can get back to performing at a higher level.

Policy # 3 Understand others will make mistakes

Remember, you are not perfect and neither are your coaches or teammates. As a team leader, if you are hypercritical of your teammates after they make a mistake, three negative things could happen. A teammate could:

- **Become defensive.** Instantly fire back with a comment about one of your mistakes.

- **Doubt him/herself.** Immediately take the criticism too seriously and start to doubt his or her abilities.

- **Retaliate.** Mentally store the comment while waiting for you to make a mistake. The teammate then criticizes you in the same way he or she was criticized.

Any of the above responses will eventually erode team spirit.

When my daughter, Abigayle, was in high school, she was on a competitive dance team. During her junior year, the team set a goal to make it to the state tournament, which had not happened in several years. In the middle of the routine, Abigayle started a high kick slightly ahead of the team. (Beyond the judges and her teammates, no one would have noticed her mistake.)

I walked outside the gym after their routine. Abigayle was walking to the locker room with her team and tears of disappointment were rolling down her face. Because I didn't notice the mistake, I gave her a hug and said, "Great job." She said, "No, dad, it wasn't a great job. I blew it. I started too soon in the first high kick series!" The tone of her voice indicated how disappointed she was in her performance. I wasn't sure what to say.

Luckily, a team leader noticed Abigayle's tears and walked up and asked, "What's wrong?" Huge tears were now flowing from my daughter's eyes as she said, "I blew it Carly. I started too soon!"

At this critical time, Carly, a team leader said, "We have all blown it. I was right next to you, and I don't think it will be a big deduction." Notice that Carly didn't act as if the mistake didn't happen. She tactfully acknowledged the mistake, but created a soft cushion for Abigayle to land on mentally. As it turned out, Carly's perspective and approach was right on—the deduction was minimal and the team ended up placing higher than they had at the previous meet. By creating a culture of understanding that everyone makes mistakes, a team avoids playing tentatively or scared.

As a leader, you will have the opportunity to help a teammate recover from a mistake by showing forgiveness, which will help them mentally reset. This approach will allow them to bounce back and have a positive impact in a practice, game, or even the season.

Policy # 4 Determine what you can fix

As an athlete, there are some things you can fix and some things you cannot. If you are not a fast runner, improving your foot speed will not happen in a week. However, if you are very close to mastering a new skill, or if you could make a few minor changes that would be the difference between success and failure, it's vital to explore making the changes.

If you remember, Policy #1 stated that you should review and evaluate your performance. It's easier to fix problem areas by incorporating logic instead of emotion. This is easier said than done.

> When emotions overshadow logic in mentally evaluating your performance or reviewing films, it's difficult for the brain to see the necessary changes.

Psychologists have found the frontal cortex of the brain controls logic, higher-level thinking, and is activated for problem-solving. The limbic part of the brain controls emotions. Dr. Christian Conte, a certified psychologist and motivational speaker, says, "These two parts of our brain normally 'bounce' off each other throughout the day. However, one system is usually more active than the other. If the limbic system —emotion control—is more active than the frontal cortex, it's difficult for a person to make a logical change as emotions are overruling logic." If you have ever tried to share a different perspective on a situation or be the devil's advocate with someone who is overly emotional, you understand what Dr. Conte is saying. The overly emotional person simply can't "see" a different perspective because they are emotionally connected to it.

Imagine going to your contact list in your phone and accidently hitting the wrong button, which causes you to dial the wrong person. The hypothetical "wrong person" will answer because you called them! They didn't know you were trying to connect with someone else. The same concept is true for athletes when receiving feedback, either from a coach or through a personal evaluation—we must press the right button to make the right connection. As we explore what areas we can fix for the next practice or performance, it's important to "dial" the logical frontal cortex and "disconnect" with the emotional limbic system. Although this is difficult, by practicing this mental shift over time, you will begin to become less emotional during critical feedback. Imagine how good you and your team could be if you and your teammates determined to fix two or three things on a weekly basis!

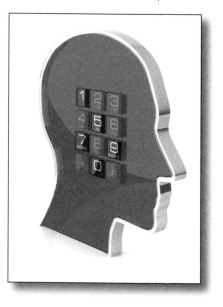

As you review your previous performance, look for the two or three things you can fix, and focus logically on connecting logically to those things during practice.

Policy # 5 Constantly look to improve

Anthony Robbins, motivational speaker and author, describes a formula that weaves into Policy #5.

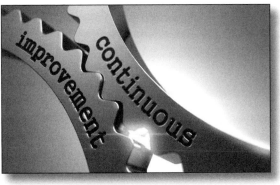

CANI:

Constant

And

Never-ending

Improvement

Whether you just played your best game ever or suffered your worst performance and lost, the CANI policy will be useful as you prepare for the next contest. CANI is powerful for individuals and teams.

To make the formula even more valuable, let's look at adding three punctuation marks after the "I" and notice how it changes the message.

Placing a period (.) after the "I" could suggest you are determined to improve—period. An exclamation point (!) after the "I" indicates you are excited about new ways to improve! A question mark (?) could mean you are asking yourself, "How can I get better?"

Q) Which punctuation mark is correct?

A) All of them.!?

Each of the five policies for bouncing back from a loss is important. To increase their value, add one four-letter word after the CANI formula and you are destined to improve.

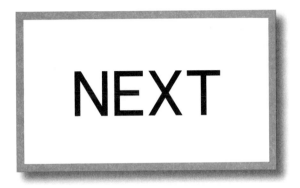

Saying, "NEXT" to yourself allows your mind to shift from focusing on the mistake to looking to the future. If you consistently follow Karl Mecklenburg's policies on rebounding from a loss or poor performance, you and your team will bounce back more quickly. This approach will also provide a better chance to win the *next* game.

"We can look back, we just can't go back!"

Rebounding from a win

Most people tend to think rebounding from a win isn't necessary. Mr. Mecklenburg made an interesting distinction during our interview regarding the importance of rebounding from a win as well as a loss. He said, "Whether you win or lose, it's important to go through the same process."

Let's go back to what Phil Jackson said about winning, "Never let winning go to your head." It happens almost every season to one team in your school. That team is destroying opponents left and right. Soon, the team is ranked in the state poll. Then all of a sudden, a team with very little talent comes along and defeats the state-ranked team.

Why does this happen? Usually because players on the team got a little too arrogant and forgot how hard they worked to create their positive result. It can also happen when a team has beaten another team for years. Arrogance is dangerous. Your job as a team leader is to keep the team confident, but not arrogant. There is a huge difference. Confidence is believing you are going to win, while arrogance is believing you can't be beat. If arrogance creeps into your team, don't be surprised if the opponent you "looked past" sneaks up and beats you.

Top leaders rebound from a loss, poor performance, or even a win like a rubber ball being dropped on a gym floor—the harder they are thrown down, the higher they bounce back!

Please go to the **Certification Packet** in section three to complete the application exercises for this chapter.

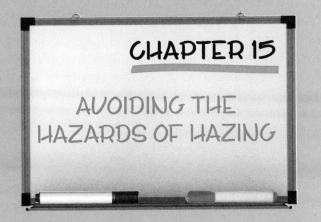

CHAPTER 15

AVOIDING THE HAZARDS OF HAZING

"Humiliation doesn't build team spirit—it destroys it."
—Craig Hillier

Hazing is a hot topic with athletic teams. Most high school teams do not participate in hazing activities. Unfortunately, there are still high school teams that participate in hazing events. Too often, upperclassmen believe hazing is just a rite of passage, and it should continue. The belief some upperclassmen hold to is if they had to go through it, so should the younger players. When the topic of hazing is brought up in my live sessions, I ask anyone who has been hazed if they enjoyed the process and thought it brought value to the team. Almost everyone says no. Most hated being humiliated. Then I ask, "If you hated it, why would you do it to someone else?" It's a difficult question for students to answer. Usually they say, "It's tradition."

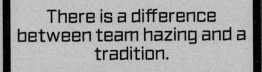

There is a difference between team hazing and a tradition.

Hazing is defined as "any humiliating or dangerous activity expected of you to join a group, regardless of your willingness to participate." Examples of hazing from the Alfred University study in New York included shaving heads, taping people to trees, or stripping a student down to his underwear and locking him out of school during a weight lifting session. Sometimes hazing even results in a student's death.

In fact, the statistics on hazing in high school sports are startling. Susan Lipkins, author of *Preventing Hazing*, has researched hazing and discovered the following facts:[1]

- Each year 1.5 million high school students are hazed.

- In high school, 91% of the students belong to at least one group, and nearly half of them–48%–report being subjected to hazing activities.

- Of the 48% who were subjected to hazing, 43% were subjected to humiliating activities, and 30% performed potentially illegal acts as part of their initiation.

- Both male and female students report high levels of hazing.

Sadly, explicit, gross, and inexcusable sexual acts and harassment are trending among hazing rituals. If you research some of the stories on this deviant behavior, your stomach will turn. It's nearly impossible to understand why someone would inflict some of these acts on their teammates.

---

[1] Lipkins, S. (2006). *Preventing hazing: How parents, teachers, and coaches can stop the violence, harassment, and humiliation.* San Francisco: Jossey-Bass.

The costs of hazing

Anyone who organizes, participates, or even watches a hazing event could be subject to loss of title, team suspension, loss of college scholarship, or even possible criminal prosecution.

When a hazing incident is reported, the first students to be called to an administrator's office will be team leaders and captains. *It is unlikely the hazing took place without a team leader's knowledge or approval.* Furthermore, one of the fastest ways to go from hero to zero is to initiate a hazing event or be at the event and not stop it. If you are a team captain, and a hazing incident takes place under your watch, you will most likely lose your captainship.

After a hazing event has been exposed, the next step usually involves suspensions or forfeits. If you participated in or witnessed a hazing event, it's common to

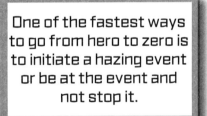

One of the fastest ways to go from hero to zero is to initiate a hazing event or be at the event and not stop it.

be suspended for several games. Many athletic directors have removed athletes for the rest of the season to show the school and community a zero tolerance stance. In fact, some nationally ranked teams have cancelled the balance of their season because of hazing. Can you imagine a stupid act putting you and your team in a national spotlight? Your school's image will be stained because of a poor decision a small group of people make.

Once a college hears that one of their recruits took part in a hazing incident, they are inclined to pull the scholarship or offer to play. Here's another question for you: Can you imagine the feeling of losing a scholarship to play at the college level because you thought it was "funny" to make another kid do something humiliating and gross?

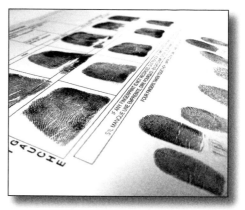

If a hazing offender is convicted of a sexual crime as an adult, which will happen starting around age 18, it can follow that person for the rest of his or her life. In some states, a hazing event that was sexual in nature creates a "sexual predator" status with law enforcement. When an individual with this status moves into a neighborhood, the entire neighborhood is alerted of this person's legal status. Think of walking down the street at your new place and having parents call their kids back into the house when they see you. In many states, the sexual predator label on your record will also follow you forever.

To be candid, it's uncomfortable to include these statistics and stories. But, I'm committed to sharing them, because I don't want you or anyone else to think hazing is all right or that it's "no big deal." Hazing IS a big deal. The consequences are even bigger.

Traditions over hazing

Traditions support the team and its members and can create unity. Traditions can be something the team has done for years that is fun and not humiliating to its new members. Examples might include dressing up during the school day for games, chanting a cheer, attending a team meal, having team breakfasts, or showing up at a movie together. Some teams donate their time to community service by adopting a highway or putting on a sports clinic for younger kids. In a community adjacent to mine, there is a go kart racing track. The go karts can go up to 40 mph. These traditions would not be considered intimidating or humiliating.

Here's a unique spin on hazing. Informally tell your teammates from the youngest grade to meet at the practice field or gym at 7 AM sharp with their tennis shoes on. Don't tell them what's going to happen. Then, show up with bagels and cream cheese for everyone. Talk about tossing out hazing and developing a strong team tradition! **These younger students will never forget how they felt** *included* **instead of** *excluded* **from the team.** And, they'll be relieved that their older classmates are doing something positive rather than demeaning. Try to think of something that will bond a team together on and off the floor of competition.

If your team has encouraged hazing in the past, it's time to stop it. Instead of hazing, create a tradition that will last for years. By adopting team traditions instead of practicing

hazing, you are putting yourself in a position to have a season of significance.

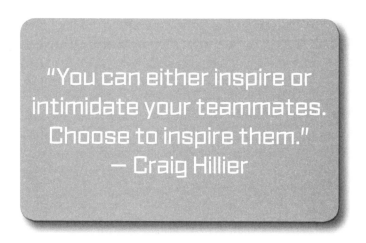

"You can either inspire or intimidate your teammates. Choose to inspire them." — Craig Hillier

Please go to the **Certification Packet** in section three to complete the application exercises for this chapter.

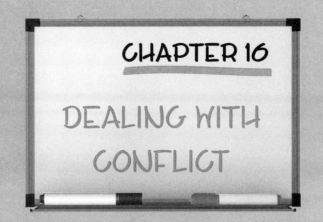

CHAPTER 16

DEALING WITH CONFLICT

"To get it right, you must see it right!"

Have you ever noticed how easy it is to be upbeat and excited when your team is performing at a top level? Teammates are laughing and smiling. They enjoy being around each other. Coaches may knock a few minutes off physical conditioning, because the past four matches have gone extremely well.

Then out of nowhere, something new and uncomfortable pops up. Suddenly, your teammates are intentionally not passing you the puck. Teammates start to laugh and whisper as you stretch out before swim practice. Maybe a loss sends your coaching staff off the deep end. The coaches verbally rip your team apart, and a few players are considering quitting in the middle of the season. Now what?

Conflict is inevitable.

You've just experienced a pitfall called conflict. How will you work through this and come out stronger? This is one area with which I had difficulty as a team leader and captain. I do not like conflict.

Too often I tried to ignore the crisis and hoped it would go away. Occasionally, that worked. But most of the time, it didn't.

This chapter gives you some ideas on working through conflict. You will learn a formula to manage conflict in a tactful way rather than losing your cool and saying things you may regret later. You will become a stronger individual and a stronger team because you had the courage to face the conflict and resolve it.

Dealing with Conflict

This chapter is titled *Dealing* with Conflict. It doesn't say *ignoring* conflict or **attacking** conflict. Let's face it, conflict is inevitable. If you put two or more people in a room together, it won't take long before a problem arises. If a problem is addressed in an assertive rather than an aggressive fashion, you and your team will be able to tackle the issue and move on. If it's not addressed appropriately, the conflict could snowball into a major crisis that divides the team and eventually makes people want to quit. Then, you find yourself losing games you should have won because the off-the-court issues were preventing you from working as a team. I've heard literally hundreds of horror stories about how conflict has destroyed teams and friendships. Sometimes the conflict or problem itself is the reason the relationship was destroyed. *But many times, it's the way people attempt to resolve the conflict that's the bigger issue.*

Most people deal with conflict in one of two ways. First, they let the problem go without addressing it, hoping it will just go away. Second, they wait until they are so irritated by it that they blow up at the person involved in the problem. Neither of these approaches works well to resolve the problem. Conflict doesn't have to be a tug of war with one winner and one loser.

Unfortunately, we get little information on how to deal constructively with conflict. I attended twelve years of school and four years of college with a major in business and a minor in speech communication, and I never had a course or even a conversation on how to deal with conflict.

The ideas in this chapter have literally changed my life. I have gone from a person who avoided conflict like a vicious disease to someone who is comfortable with conflict. That doesn't mean that I like conflict, but I'm more comfortable with it because of the distinctions I've learned.

Start Right

We typically deal with conflict based on how the authority figures in our lives deal with conflict. Authority figures can include parents, stepparents, neighbors, coaches, and teachers. If no one taught these adults effective strategies for managing conflict, and they handle conflict in a poor fashion, we could continue the pattern by default.

So, what's the best way to deal with conflict? Too often people think you should address conflict as soon as it happens—no matter where you are. If you have a problem or conflict with a teammate or coach, do you bring it up in front of a large group or while the whole team is watching? No! At least not at the beginning of the conflict. Could there be a time when several people want to address the issue and the only way to do that is in the presence of the entire group? Sure. But think about a time when you had someone jump on your case in front of a large group. Did you feel comfortable or uncomfortable? It's an uneasy feeling having a group stare at you while someone is in your face about an issue.

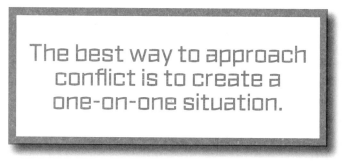

The best way to approach conflict is to create a one-on-one situation.

Tell the person that you want to talk privately. It's a lot easier to create a comfortable atmosphere when only two people are involved.

The Right Tone

After you've established the one-on-one setting, think about your tone of voice. Have you ever read a text from a friend and said to yourself, "I can't believe they would say that!" You interpreted the meaning with a certain critical or negative tone in your head.

Furthermore, you've probably talked back to your parents, and they responded with, "Watch your mouth!" Maybe you responded in the way most teens have in such situations. You responded in a much different, positive tone saying, "What? All I said was...." Then you smiled and thought you had talked your way out of it. You've done that, haven't you? The tone of your voice plays a major role in dealing with conflict.

What kind of tone should you have? *It's better to be curious, not accusatory.* If you approach the person like a detective who is humbly trying to figure out a problem, you will have an excellent chance of dealing with the situation. With a non-accusatory tone, the other person is more likely to open up. Getting in someone's face and yelling in a harsh voice, "What's your problem?" will not work. When you resort to force, that's usually what you'll get back. When you fight fire with fire, you just get a bigger fire. By taking a curious tone you will be able to put out the fire of conflict and preserve your relationship.

Perspective

Quick question.

Is this illustration concave or convex?

In other words, does
the line curve in or curve out?

Your perspective will determine
if it curves in or out.

If you look at the curved line from the left, the illustration curves away, which is considered convex. If you looked at the line from the right, it curves in toward you and is considered concave. Your mental perspective determines how and what you see.

Doesn't the same thing happen in conflict? What "side" do we normally take when we have an issue with someone? Most people admit that they only look at their side of a conflict and either don't see or ignore the other person's perspective. Almost 100% of the time, we play a part in the conflict. One of the habits in Stephen Covey's incredible book, *The 7 Habits of Highly Effective People* is First, seek to understand—then be understood. This approach is more about finding a solution than proving someone wrong. If your goal is to prove someone wrong by intimidation or humiliation, you may prove a point, but you'll lose the relationship.

Instead of having to be "right," do your best to see things from your perspective, **and** from the other person's perspective. Remember—the curved line was both concave and convex. It's very possible you are not as "right" as you think you are. Let's look at the OTFDN formula, which focuses on finding a solution, not finding fault.

The OTFDN Formula

The OTFDN formula has an immense impact on how to deal with conflict. When I teach this formula in a live session, I present it as a mnemonic device, which is a unique story that incorporates the letters in the formula. Mnemonic devices are very helpful when trying to remember a strategy or skill long term.

The mnemonic device for dealing with conflict the OTFDN way is easy to remember, think: *Open The Front Door Now.* When you think of those words, they create a picture in your mind of opening the door and addressing the problem in a tactful fashion.

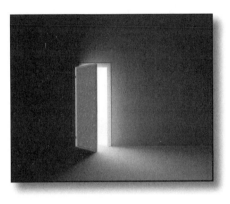

Once you know the effective tone of voice, and you've found a private place to discuss the problem, it's time to use the "O" in the OTFDN formula.

"O" stands for observation

Let's say a teammate has been late for practice the past three days. This is frustrating for the coaching staff and the rest of the team. It's not respectful, nor is it promoting team unity. Now it's time to address the problem.

You might say something like, "I've noticed that you've been late for practice the past three days." You're stating what you have seen or observed. This is an assertive way of addressing the problem. It's not threatening, but it's not timid either.

"T" stands for thoughts

The next part of the exchange might sound like this, "I'm curious to get your thoughts on that." Why do you want to get this person's thoughts on the issue when that person is creating the problem? You may not have all the facts. Maybe that person knows something you don't know.

Have you ever had someone verbally attack you without giving you a chance to explain your side of the story? That is a disheartening approach. It's vital to get the person's thoughts on the issue, because it will determine how you'll proceed.

If the teammate says, "My parents are at work, and my grandpa's medical aide is on vacation, so I've been running home to make sure he gets his medication," you're going to back off and take a softer approach. That satisfactorily explains why your teammate has been late.

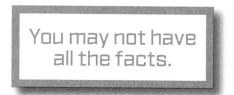

You may not have all the facts.

If instead the teammate says, "Yeah, I know I was late. I was just talking with some friends, and the time got away from me," this excuse doesn't cut it. By asking for the person's thoughts in a detective-like fashion, you are attempting to figure out what is going through this person's head regarding the problem or situation. Now it's time to use the "F" in the formula.

"F" stands for feedback

At this point you get a chance to give your feedback on the situation. Explain how this person's actions are affecting you or the team. If the teammate had said he was racing home to help a sick grandparent (or something similar), you might say, "Wow, I wish you would have told me. What can I do to help?" The feedback you give shows your concern for your teammate and his situation.

If the teammate had said he was just talking with some friends, proceed with caution. This is delicate. You don't want to rip into the person, yet you don't want to dance around the issue.

In this situation, you might say, "I just wanted you to know that everyone on the team, including me, is frustrated by your late arrival. It looks like you don't respect the coaches or the people who are there on time."

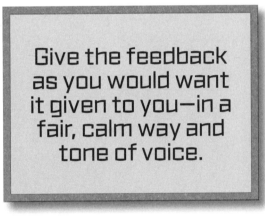

Give the feedback as you would want it given to you—in a fair, calm way and tone of voice.

After you have covered the feedback phase, the two of you probably will talk some more. This feedback should shed some light on the person's actions. Often, people have no idea how their actions affect others. When you're finished giving each other feedback, move to the "D" in the formula.

"D" stands for desire

Clearly state what you want to change. It may sound something like, "I really want you to show up on time so that we have a great practice from start to finish." Watch for the person's response. If the person is nodding in agreement, move to the "N" in the formula. If you sense the person disagrees with you, go back to the observation phase and continue the conversation.

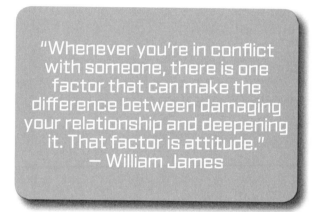

"Whenever you're in conflict with someone, there is one factor that can make the difference between damaging your relationship and deepening it. That factor is attitude."
— William James

"N" stands for next time

Once the two of you agree on what needs to change, lay the groundwork for the next time this situation arises. If the teammate was late because he was taking care of a sick grandparent you might say, "The next time you have to get home right after school because of a family issue, please text me so that I can pass along that information to the coach."

If you're dealing with the teammate who was late because he was just talking with friends, you might say, "Next time this happens, the coach may not let you start the game." Use the phrase "next time" because it lays out the consequence if the person repeats the offense.

This formula works in a variety of situations. Let's say your coach has been rude and difficult to be around for the past few days. Approach your coach after practice and use the OTFDN formula. Say something like, "Coach, you don't seem to be yourself the past few days. You've been ranting and raving a lot, and I just wanted to get your thoughts on that." By taking this assertive approach, you will find almost every coach will explain what's going on.

Delicate Playing Time Issue

Let's look at another situation that causes conflict and apply the OTFDN method. Maybe you are in a situation where the amount of playing time is less than what you expected. You find yourself frustrated and confused as to why you are not playing more. It's easy for the frustration to build up and affect your performance in practice. It's also common to try too hard once you are playing to prove the point.

You may have teammates and even parents saying, "You are getting ripped off. I can't understand why 'so and so' is playing ahead of you." It's easy to let the frustration of the situation get the best of you. Suddenly, emotion takes over and you find yourself making negative comments in practice or in the locker room. Or even worse, you confront the coach in a loud voice saying something such as, "Everyone knows I should be playing more. You just play your favorites. You don't know what you're doing."

As a coach and parent, I have never seen this approach work. Normally, this outburst takes things from bad to worse. And, having a parent contact a coach to discuss playing time is also not a good idea. Parents may not like or agree with the amount of time you are playing, but attempting to confront or persuade the coach to play you more is not a good idea. It's not your parents' responsibility to have the conversation with the coach if you feel slighted on playing time.

Normally, coaches respect the fact that you had enough courage to discuss an issue with them directly instead of talking about it with everyone except them. If you approach the difficult conversation of playing time correctly, you will gain insight from your coach's perspective and allow your coach to hear your side of the story.

Here's how it may go:

(Athlete in blue—**Coach in bold black italics.**)

Make sure you are approaching the discussion at an appropriate time, potentially after practice.

Coach, do you have a few minutes?

"I have two minutes, what's up?"

In the event the coach has another commitment and is rushed, this is not the time for the conversation. A rushed conversation dealing with a delicate conversation is a recipe for failure. If the coach doesn't have the time when you approach her, say…

"I've got a few things on my mind and I understand you have to run. When would you have 15 minutes?"

"How about tomorrow after practice?"

If that works on your end, agree to the time. The next day after practice, make sure you are in a spot where the conversation isn't going to be overheard.

"This is a little awkward and uncomfortable. I feel I owe it to you and to myself to have a conversation with you directly. It seems like I have not been playing as much as I expected." (Observation.) "Can you give me your thoughts and feedback on this?" (In this situation, you are combining Thoughts and Feedback.)

At this point, it's vital to be aware of your body language. If you have crossed arms and are leaning back in a chair, you are sending a message of being closed off. Instead, make direct eye contact, relax your arms at your side, breathe evenly, and mentally think, "I want to try to figure out what's going on. This works better than thinking "The coaches don't know what they are doing."

Let's assume the coach says something like this: "I appreciate you bringing this to me instead of keeping it to yourself and getting frustrated. Here's the deal,

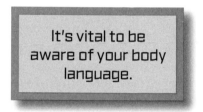

It's vital to be aware of your body language.

you're an important member of this team. You bring a lot in practice and in a game. However, there are a few things that prevent you from seeing more playing time. First, I sometimes get the impression in practice you think some of the drills we are doing are dumb, and it doesn't look like you are giving 100%. Others see this and then they follow by giving the same effort you are giving. In the past, I've seen you go 100% in these drills, and it's pretty clear you are not doing that very much anymore."

You may not like or agree with what was just said, and it may be tempting to argue the point. Instead of arguing however, it would be better to acknowledge the feedback and pledge to improve: "OK, I can improve on that."

The coach may then say, "You are also not as strong at (skill) as (other player)." Again, you may not agree.

Avoid defensive comments. Instead, it would be better to say, "I appreciate the feedback. My desire is to improve and help the team win more games. If I work harder in practice during drills and work on (skill), do you see me playing more?" It's unlikely a coach will say, "yes," because there are other variables you are not even aware of. Ideally, the coach says, "Probably."

By hearing a "probably" by the end of this OTFD... exchange, you just had an awesome breakthrough. You now have clarity on where you stand, why you are not playing as much as you wanted, and specifically what you need to work on to improve.

BUT...Don't forget the N! True leaders are willing to be held accountable. To incorporate the N in the OTFDN conversation, say something such as: "Coach, next time it looks like I'm not giving 100% in drills, give me some sort of sign so I know to pick it up." You may want to end the conversation by saying: "Thanks for hearing me out on this, coach. I feel a lot better now, and I just want our team to have the best season possible."

When I present this scenario in a workshop with coaches and athletes, I openly ask the coaches to share their feedback. Without exception the coaches say, ***"That's exactly how I'd like my athletes to handle the conversation on playing time."***

"Take the feedback without the push back."

Mediating Conflict

As a team leader, it's your obligation to be a conflict manager whether you like this role or not. Throughout the season, challenges will arise that require your mediation. This isn't easy. It's tempting to just ignore the conflict in hopes it will disappear.

Don't let small issues build until they get out of control and break your team bond. If you have a problem with a coach or teammate, be strong enough to address the situa-  tion. Do it as soon as possible. Remember: you may not have all the facts. You could be making an unfair or inaccurate conclusion based on limited knowledge. You can still use the OTFDN formula when working through an issue between two of your teammates.

> "Conflict is drama, and how people deal with conflict shows you the kind of people they are."
> – Stephen Moyer

Although the OTFDN formula is effective, it is not 100%. Sometimes you can't work through the conflict, but at least you had the courage to try to resolve it. Team leaders are wise enough to understand that sometimes people are going to disagree. But you can come to an agreement on that—agree to disagree. There will be times when both sides will see the other's perspective, but neither will compromise their position. You can still have a season of significance even if everyone doesn't agree all the time. It's rare to have complete harmony on a team.

I promise you that the OTFDN formula will help you manage conflict in a positive manner. You will be able to use this formula not only with teammates and coaches but in every relationship you have. Conflict is inevitable. Deal with it effectively and then move on!

Please go to the **Certification Packet** in section three to complete the application exercises for this chapter.

"An eye for an eye will only make the whole world blind."

— Mahatma Gandhi

CHAPTER 17

MANAGING SOCIAL MEDIA

"Whether via social media or in person, building your relationships is a long–term process, and the ultimate goal is to strengthen your network one person at a time."
—Raymond Arroyo

Everyone, regardless of age or social connections, is or can be affected by the tidal wave of today's social media phenomena. Think about the following real-world scenarios.

→ A fan of a popular singer posts he is looking forward to an upcoming concert and would love to get a picture with the star. After the concert, the singer tweets instructions to head over to security for a back stage pass. The fan and a handful of others are escorted to the bus where they hang out with the singer before the bus drives off to the next city.

→ A dynamic 16-year-old leader loses her life in an auto accident. One of her leadership missions was to gather and donate 1,000 books for an inner city school. After her untimely death, a small group of friends keep her dream alive by posting and tweeting that the book drive will continue. Community members, even those with no connection to the young woman, multiplied the effort by retweeting, sharing the story on Facebook, and linking the mission to their social media networks. The drop-off site didn't receive 1,000 books. Instead, 4,750 books were donated! Even today, the drive continues with all new books going to different parts of the world.

➔ A sharp 11th grade student athlete—known as funny, outgoing, and drug and alcohol free, is at a party where students are drinking. Someone asks him to hand them a beer from the cooler. He sets down the soda he is drinking and grabs the beer. At that exact moment, someone snaps a photo of him with their phone, which is then posted online and is forwarded to the athletic director. Although the student didn't consume any alcohol, the athletic director makes the difficult decision to suspend the student. The school policy states that anyone suspended for a drinking violation is not eligible to be a team captain. The young man not only sits out 25% of the athletic season, but he is no longer eligible to become a team captain even though he was destined to be one his senior year.

➔ A group of boys talk an 8th grade girl into taking pictures of another girl while she is changing for PE in exchange for $5. She takes the photos and texts them to the boys, who immediately forward the pictures to all their contacts. Within two hours, all parties have been rounded up by the police liaison and school administration and are informed the photos could be considered pornography. The painstaking process of removing the photos from hundreds of phones begins. Eventually, all infected phones are cleaned up, and after the punishment is handed out, life moves on—sort of. The girl who took the photos can't live down her mistake and the girl violated by the prank wonders if all the photos are really gone.

 It's a jungle out there! Social media refers to interaction among people in which they create, share, or exchange information and ideas in virtual communities and networks. Social media is booming; in fact, there are hundreds of sites that collectively host millions of users worldwide. While social media has value, purpose, and positive qualities, it also presents opportunities for pitfalls.

It's no secret that schools want to be known for how their athletes and teams are creating a season of significance. They can do without the social media nightmares that often create a negative firestorm in their school, among their teams, and in the community.

This chapter covers four fundamental factors of social media and outlines the POST formula for managing social media posts effectively.

Fundamental Factors of Social Media:

1. The meaning of text is up for debate.
2. Don't count on being anonymous.
3. Everything sent or posted is potentially permanent.
4. What you say or post is a reflection of who you are.

The meaning of text is up for debate.

Take a simple, six-word statement, "I didn't say he liked her." How many different meanings does this sentence imply? Just by emphasizing each word independently, you can produce six meanings. Now add voice inflection, body language, and a person's personality, and the simple statement has dozens of meanings. It's easy to jump to conclusions when interpreting text because the tone of the text can't be "read." Remember this when you post or text. The nature of social media, and the wide range of people who may read your posts, multiplies the possible interpretations of the words you type.

Don't count on being anonymous.

Several social media sites promote anonymous content. They usually feature things such as:

- Saucy questions posed to a large group

- Inappropriate comments about others

- False rumors designed to create drama

It's both amazing and scary to see how brave one can be behind the shield of presumed anonymity. However, many people have discovered their anonymous post gets tracked back to them, and with today's technology, it's not difficult to do so if necessary. For example a high-ranking political staff member was stung by an *anonymous* Twitter account he created that constantly questioned his superior's decisions. The Twitter feed leaked vital, sensitive information to the media. When the comments were traced, he lost his job. Of course, finding his next job will be challenging to say the least. It's very difficult to remain anonymous in our hyper-connected world.

Everything sent or posted is potentially permanent.

Think of a social media post like a tattoo. Many people are easily drawn into a tattoo shop or a social media site because such locations, whether brick-and-mortar  or virtual, are trendy and popular. We see a design that catches our eye and decide to press *send*, authorizing the ink to be injected into our skin. Ask anyone who has had a tattoo, and they will tell you about both the pain and the rush. Most of the time, the tattoo is considered a success because the look they desired is now on their body. It's a decision they'll see for the rest of their life. Unfortunately, sometimes tattoos are done poorly or are no longer desirable. The tattoo can be covered by a larger tattoo or a person can attempt to remove it through expensive, painful laser sessions. Either approach will be agonizing. Any post, including photos, videos, text, instant messages—even videos that supposedly disappear after a few seconds—can potentially be captured and reposted. While deleting an unwanted tattoo (post) is possible, it's going to take a lot of time, effort, and expense.

What you say or post is a reflection of who you are.

We are all familiar with the broadcast stations ABC, CBS, NBC, and ESPN. Today, every individual who participates in social media becomes a broadcaster on a brand new station known as Y—O—U. Just as any news program determines what will be shown to their audience, we do the same on  our news station. Whenever we forward, link, or share content it can be viewed as though we endorse or have authored the material. If we post a funny video we find on YouTube, we essentially say, "I find this funny, and I believe you will too." If we link a statement about faith, family, or facts, we are advertising that statement from our personal broadcast company. When a friend *forwards* or *posts* something, have you ever thought, "Wow, I can't believe they're putting their name next to that!"? If so, you understand the reflection concept. While the content may originate from a third party, it's now being broadcast on your station. Furthermore, it's important to remember comments you post about content will play a vital role in how your audience perceives the post or perceives you as an individual. With the understanding that the meaning of any text can be debated, it's vital to decide what content you broadcast from your station.

When you understand the four fundamental factors of social media, we can use and leverage it as an asset rather than a liability. With any technology, there are ways to use it to benefit society, and there are ways it can be a burden to society.

Using the POST social media formula

- **P**roduce and promote positive, clear, and clean posts.

- **O**bliterate any garbage from your social media station.

- **S**ee each other eye-to-eye for difficult conversations.

- **T**hink before pressing **send**.

Produce and promote positive, clear, and clean posts.

Too often, athletes at all levels lash out at how a game was officiated, challenge a coach's decision, or slam the game environment. While there may be a small sense of relief by a "got that off my back!" comment said in frustration, the boomerang effect is now in play. Typically, a wave of controversy and distraction are headed toward the player making the comment. After speaking out, there are now two issues. The first issue is defending or attempting to recant the comment said in the heat of the moment. The second issue is the distraction a team faces as a result of the post or comment.

I've seen dozens of examples when athletes who just lost a close contest go to social media and write,

"It was a tough loss for us. I'd like to thank the fans for showing up. We are going to look at our mistakes, go back to practice, and get better. We hope to have the chance to redeem ourselves next week."

By producing and promoting clear, clean, and positive posts, a negative tidal wave is avoided. It's short, upbeat, and to the point. Being positive, clear, and clean, does not provide others with ammunition to fuel a fire.

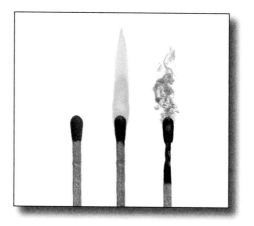

Positive, clear, and clean posts should also be a part of your *posting philosophy*. You may be ticked off at a friend or a situation where you are being treated unfairly. Be wise enough to keep it to yourself. You'll prevent the situation from escalating.

Two students from a high school in southeast Minnesota recently started a Twitter account to which only positive messages could be posted. Several administrators know the students who oversee the account and are followers on Twitter as well. In a phone interview for this chapter with the students who manage the account, they were amazed at the positive vibe the Twitter feed created in the school. They told me stories of students congratulating other students on concert and band performances; commenting on strong efforts in sports even though the team lost; and thanking people for going out of their way to be kind when they could have just kept walking down the hallway. Although no negative comments have been posted, the two student administrators are prepared to message the sender *directly* that the unflattering post will not go into the Twitter feed.

Obliterate any "garbage" from your social media broadcast station.

Webster's dictionary de-
fines "obliterate" as *re-*
moving or destroying
completely. As part of the
college recruiting process,
coaching assistants are re-
questing to be *friends* with
or *follow* their recruits on
social media. If this request

is not accepted, an unspoken signal is sent that says, "I don't want you looking at my broadcast station." If coaches antic-ipate a problem with a high school recruit in the process, it is unlikely they will pursue the athlete. And, in the corporate world, many companies explore a job candidate's social me-dia during the interview process. If they see photos or posts illustrating questionable behavior, they move on quickly to the next candidate. If your broadcast station is littered with garbage, get to work and clean it out now. If undesirable content can't be deleted through a personal request by or asking the host site to eliminate it, consider employing a reputation restoration company. At times, the weight of their request gets quicker action. A reputation company may also employ technology and strategies to push down the questionable content.

See each other eye-to-eye during difficult conversations.

When you need to have a difficult conversation, it's tempting to take the easy, relatively stress-free approach of texting. It may appear more comfortable to take this approach because you can't hear someone yelling at you in a text, UNLESS THEY USE ALL CAPS! And, even seeing ALL CAPS sometimes seems more attractive than a loud voice. Some people choose this approach because it gives them time to respond during a heated discussion. While there are a few minor advantages to using text during a difficult conversation, too often it can go wrong.

By understanding the fundamental factor that the meaning of text is up for debate, it's very common to assume a negative tone when reading text during a conflict. Furthermore, it's easy to avoid responding to a text and ignore the conflict. Certainly, some face-to-face conversations get heated, and walking away is the best approach. Most of the time, however, people don't walk away when they are discussing an issue face-to-face.

A high school senior shared a story with me along this line. Her boyfriend was in a foul mood and looking for a squabble. The back-and-forth texts between the two started to become mean-spirited. The girl texted, "I'm gonna say goodbye now." Because she was upset, she went to the gym to work out, leaving her phone in a locker. When she returned, she sees 15 texts, eight missed calls, and four voice mails. Each text became meaner; each voicemail message became more and more furious. The young woman then visits her boyfriend's Twitter account and sees his post ranting about his "immature" girlfriend. Both of their Twitter followers started asking questions, taking sides, and calling each other out.

This example shows that a small disagreement between two people can suddenly turn into a large group mess! All of this could have been avoided by having the discussion face-to-face. No doubt face-to-face discussions during difficult conversations are uncomfortable and nerve-racking; however, almost all of the time they are more productive than attempting to resolve an issue via text.

Think before you hit "send."

If you examine the stories of social media gone wrong, you'll see one common thread. People didn't think about the whole range of potential consequences before pressing "send." At times, it's difficult to imagine the negative impact of a single post. Think back to elementary school when the concept of addition was relatively easy to understand. You picked up on it quickly because an illustration of blocks showed you two plus three equals five. Yet, do you remember how difficult it was to understand multiplication? You couldn't see it. It was a mystery. The only way to "get it" was to memorize the multiplication chart. Even though your memorization taught you that 9 x 6 was 54, you weren't sure why!

Social media has the same multiplying, mysterious effect. Why does one post, either positive or negative, go viral, whereas another similar post is read by only two people? No one can answer that question. The

multiplying effect of social media is mind blowing. Sometimes the silliest content goes worldwide, while other life-changing content remains dormant in social media.

Before pressing send on any social media outlet, ask yourself a few questions.

- ➡ Is what I'm about to post helpful or hurtful?

- ➡ What potential issues could I face if this content is released or forwarded?

- ➡ Am I upset? Am I trying to get back at someone with this post?

- ➡ Am I okay with this content being out there for the rest of my life?

- ➡ Is this worthy of broadcast from Channel Y—O—U?

> "Don't say anything online that you wouldn't want plastered on a billboard with your face on it." — Erin Bury, Sprouter community manager

If you run through these questions and are comfortable and confident with your answers, it's probably okay to press send. If not, have the courage, compassion, and composure to wait. Most likely, the waiting period will have you either editing the post or not posting at all. Thinking before you press send may save you an incredible amount of heartache.

Social media is not going away. It's here to stay. It can be an incredible tool to impact lives in a positive way. It can also be a tool that can be detrimental. At the core of social media, we must understand a simple concept: either we manage it, or it manages us!

> "Monitor, engage, and be transparent; these have always been the keys to success in the digital space."
> — Dallas Lawrence, Levick Strategic Communications

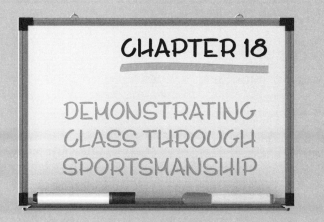

CHAPTER 18

DEMONSTRATING CLASS THROUGH SPORTSMANSHIP

"Win or lose, we will be a class act." — Coach Rick Ellingworth, Craig Hillier's high school football coach

With a two-goal deficit and a handful of seconds left in a hockey game, the losing team starts a fistfight. The winners are slated to advance to the state tournament. The individuals who started it are seniors and are not concerned about a suspension.

A college softball player hits a home run but tears her ACL as she leaves the batter's box. The rules state a batter must touch all the bases for the home run to count. Two young women, *on the opposing team*, carry her around the field so she can gently tag each base.

In each of these situations, the opponent had a choice— be full of class or be class*less*.

Too often, teams of all ages and levels of play are taking the classless route.

Our entire world is suffering from poor sportsmanship, not just in athletics. Drive down a freeway and watch people respond when they get cut off or when someone needs to make a lane change in order to reach an exit. It's disheartening to see the finger gestures and anger that occur over basically harmless acts. Even airlines are battling air rage where passengers waiting for a late flight become violent toward airline employees. Schools are seeing more students in the classroom verbally blow up after receiving a bad grade. In short, we need to commit to sportsmanship on and off the floor of competition.

What is Sportsmanship?

Sportsmanship boils down to:

→ Playing by the rules.

→ Accepting the official's calls.

→ Committing to being a class act regardless of the competition's outcome.

There are several aspects of sportsmanship. Unfortunately, some of these areas you have little control over. These include the behavior of opponents, fans, and opposing coaches. It's nearly impossible to control other people's behavior. However, you can influence their behavior. There is little you can do to influence the opponent's sportsmanship, but you can choose how you and your team respond and react to various situations.

Sportsmanship means committing to be a class act regardless of the circumstances. This is a skill you can use for the rest of your life. People who are class acts gain admiration from others. They draw others in. They look at the big picture regarding their approach to life and their sport. They don't get too high with their success or fall apart when they face failure.

Top-notch teams, leaders and athletes demonstrate the CLASS formula.

- **C**ool heads prevail
- **L**ose with dignity
- **A**void arrogance
- **S**ucceed with grace
- **S**ee the big picture

Cool Heads Prevail

How many times have you witnessed an athlete completely lose it? A hot-headed athlete rants and raves about a call or becomes unglued over an opponent's remark or gesture. The player then says something inappropriate that rattles the team, coach, or fans. As a result, a technical foul is issued. If this behavior continues, the athlete is removed from the game.

A group of young men were gathered around me at a workshop in Michigan and shared a story about one of their friends who lost his composure during a very close game. Apparently, he fouled an opponent who was driving the lane for a layup. As the ball fell through the net, he punched the ball to the wall in frustration. This action led to a technical foul that added an additional free throw after the free throw awarded for the initial foul. The technical foul also gave the ball to the opposing team after the second free throw. The player who was fouled made both free throws **and** then hit a three-pointer when the ball was inbounded after the technical foul. "It was a seven-point swing in less than eight seconds," the boys told me. By not keeping a cool head, one player put his team in a difficult situation. They went on to lose the game.

The cost of an unsportsmanlike conduct foul is too high!

Leaders must keep their cool despite the urge to explode. In Richard Carlson's book, *Don't Sweat the Small Stuff*, he talks about being the eye of the tornado. The eye is the center of the tornado, and it's totally calm. The winds may be gusting at a hundred miles per hour, but the eye remains calm. Great leaders focus on staying in the eye of the storm. They understand that losing their cool will not help the team.

"Part of being a champ is acting like a champ. You have to learn how to win and not run away when you lose. Everyone has bad stretches and real successes. Either way, you have to be careful not to lose your confidence or get too confident."—Nancy Kerrigan

Lose with dignity

No one likes to lose. It's easy to come up with excuses or blame the officials.

Officials are human. They will make mistakes every now and then. Although you can't control a bad call, you can control your response to a bad call.

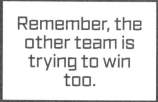

Remember, the other team is trying to win too. While you certainly shouldn't be happy after a loss, it's all right to give them some credit for winning.

There will also be times when you were simply unlucky and unfortunately you have to deal with it. I read an article about Rachel, from Pennsylvania, who was running in the 100-hurdle event at the season-ending conference meet. After the race started, the officials realized the automated timing system was not functioning, and three shots were fired in the air signaling the racers to stop running. With all the excitement, none of the hurdlers heard the shots and ran full speed to the

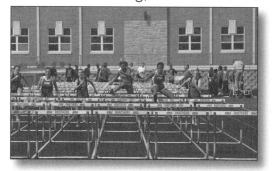

finish line. Rachel crossed the line first for an apparent victory.

With no official time recorded, officials and coaches decided to give the runners 30 minutes to recover, and they would run the race again.

Most girls were able to rest and recover before the make-up race. Rachel was also a long jumper and made two successful jumps while the hurdlers were preparing to race again. The extra effort from the high jump took a toll on her energy, and she ended up taking 8th place in the do-over race. Of course she was disappointed with the outcome, but she did not freak out about the automated timer glitch from the first race.

Saquon, who won a gold medal in the same event for the boys' team, saw what happened and recognized her as she held his starting block during his gold medal victory. The next thing he did showed an incredible amount of class. He walked up to her and according to the article, he said, "It's really hard to explain, but something inside of me told me it would be the right thing to do to give her my medal. Honestly, I love winning races and getting medals, but I felt she deserved it too. Everyone saw that girl win the race."

When asked how she felt about receiving the award, the young woman said, "It was one of the kindest things anyone's ever done."

The article indicated Rachel wasn't yelling or screaming about how the officials blew it and cost her the medal. Instead, she was dealing with it the best she could despite the officials' error. While Saquon's medal was symbolic of the victory, it was also symbolic of being a class act, and Rachel will never forget.

Avoid Arrogance

Have you ever competed against a team that gave you the impression they were going to destroy you without any effort at all? Maybe members from the other team emerged from the locker room, smirked, and made smart-aleck comments at your team during warm-ups. They acted like the game was over before it even started.

If you've ever competed against a team like that and won, you know the incredible feeling of taking those players down a notch or two. At the moment of victory, it's tempting to give them a taste of their own medicine, maybe smirk back or make some retaliatory comments as you are shaking hands after the game. Don't do it!

Commit to being a class act. Don't do the very thing you despised in the first place. Players on the other team know how they acted. They probably feel stupid now that they lost, as they should. In a situation like that, top-notch teams shake hands and celebrate in the locker room.

It's easy to get caught up in the hype of a rivalry and start to believe the other team is the enemy. They're not. The other team is your opponent. This is an important distinction. Competition is great when it brings out the best in us. However, if you have a long history of playing against an opponent, and it hasn't been a friendly exchange, sometimes teams begin to act like they would do anything to destroy the other team. When this happens, it can get ugly quickly.

Succeed with grace

Let's say you're playing a team twice during a season. The first game was played in your high school, and you won. After the game, you and your teammates pumped your fists with joy and pointed to the scoreboard to rub in the final results.

When you visit your opponent's school for your next match-up, you may have set yourself up for a disaster. The players will remember how you acted. If you lose, the other team and its fans will most likely make a huge deal about the win. The lesson: keep a win in perspective. Enjoy it. Then start to prepare for the next match-up.

Sportsmanship is demonstrated in the stands as well. **At** times you will be in the stands supporting a team from your school. As you read in Chapter 13, Setting the Stage, you represent your school and team at all times. I've heard countless stories regarding poor leadership from the student body. For example, one article told the story of a school with a high socio-economic status. When they were losing to a neighboring school perceived to be "on the wrong side of the tracks" the students chanted, "Your mom works for my dad."

In another example, an athletic director sent me an article on his disappointment and amazement when the girls' basketball team was narrowly defeated in a regional tournament. The hosting school began the "There is the losing team!" chant. If you are not familiar with this chant, one student yells out, "Where is the scoreboard?" after which the rest of the fans point to the scoreboard and yell, "There is the scoreboard!" The series of questions continues until the last question is posed: "Where is the losing team?" The audience then points to the squad that lost.

These are examples of poor sportsmanship from the fans. There are also examples of poor sportsmanship during and after a contest where athletes don't shake hands after a loss. Or, when they are shaking hands, the winners are rubbing the victory in their opponents' face. I've heard of individuals throwing sucker punches during a post-game handshaking line as well.

As an audience member in the stands or as a participating athlete, how you respond to a victory says a lot about your school and what you and your team stands for beyond the scoreboard.

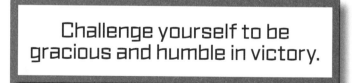

Challenge yourself to be gracious and humble in victory.

See the big picture

Check out the size of this dot.

Compared to the size of this dot.

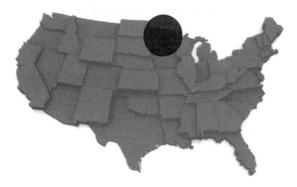

The size of the dot is the same. The perspective from which we see it changes everything.

I can remember sitting in the locker room after losing a very close basketball game to a team we really wanted to beat. All of us were just sitting on a bench staring at our lockers. The disappointment was evident on everyone's face. Normally, in these situations, the less that is said, the better. For anyone who has ever lost a game they really wanted to win, it's difficult to find words that make you feel better.

Our coach said, "Guys, we all really wanted that one. We were close to getting it. If the ball bounced a different way, it was ours. It hurts now and it's okay for it to hurt now, as it shows you care. Just remember, there are a billion people on the other side of the world who don't care. The sun will come out tomorrow, fellas, and we still have another chance to beat them at their place in a month. Let's have this loss become our fuel. I'll see you at practice on Monday."

It was short and to the point. There was no need to replay what we should have done. We would review all of that on Monday. Our coach was wise enough to read his players and give us the right words. Team leaders can play a major role in putting things in the right perspective.

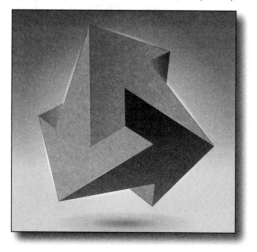

Be a
CLASS
act all the
time!

Sportsmanship is a skill you can demonstrate even after graduating from high school. There will be thousands of opportunities to show positive sportsmanship in your career. It could happen when a friend gets the job both of you wanted. If you are in a business setting, and a client decides to end your service contract and go with a competitor, you can slam the competitor or be a class act and perhaps earn the business back in the future. Maybe you become a parent, and your child was on the wrong end of an official's call. Instead of yelling at the official, it becomes the opportunity to demonstrate sportsmanship. This happens by keeping a cool head, putting the situation in the right perspective, and teaching your son or daughter about losing with dignity.

"We all like to win, but enjoy the moments along the way, no matter the outcome. Just put your heart and soul into it, and give 110%. If you do this, you will always be a winner to the person who counts most...you!"

—Marlene Blaszcyk

NOTES

NOTES

NOTES

Team Captain Section

Welcome to the team captain section! This section is designed to be a guide for team captains, but has many additional leadership lessons included for team leaders and up-and-coming leaders.

As you read earlier, there are several perspectives regarding the roles and responsibilities captains may have on a team. Some coaches view a team captain as an extension of the coaching staff. Other coaches name team captains based more on tradition and assign few responsibilities to them. There is no universal standard for team captains.

The team captain section will provide specific content beyond the team leader section. Elected or selected team captains have additional responsibilities including:

- Becoming a go-to person for a variety of decisions

- Discussing difficult issues with the coaching staff regarding current team spirit or strategies for an upcoming game or practice

- Working with vendors such as photographers, T-shirt printers, and restaurants

- Communicating with parents about upcoming events that require volunteers

- Planning pre-game meals

- Finding inspirational content for the team

- Designing team posters and promotions

- Planning camps/clinics for younger athletes

- Managing various extra duties assigned by the coaching staff

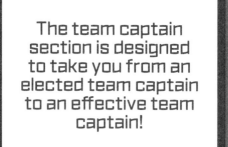

The team captain section is designed to take you from an elected team captain to an effective team captain!

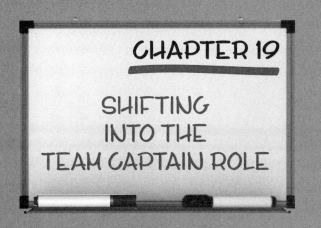

CHAPTER 19

SHIFTING INTO THE TEAM CAPTAIN ROLE

"It's not about you!" — Craig Hillier

In Chapter 3 of the team leader section, you learned about the qualities of an emerging leader. The advanced qualities outlined in this chapter will help you shift from a team leader to a team captain.

Advanced Quality #1 Serving

One of my first jobs in high school was being a server in a restaurant. I liked the job, because it involved working with people. Plus, if I performed well, guests would leave a tip. During my initial training, the manager said, "If you want to be a successful server, you must put the customer first." At times, that  meant the cooks had to prepare a dish that was not on the menu for a guest with a dietary restriction. My goal as a waiter was to do everything possible to insure the dining experience was memorable for the customers. I knew if I went out of my way to serve the customer, my tip would be larger.

Being a team captain is similar to being a server in a restaurant. The goal is to create an experience that is memorable for your customers, or in this case, teammates. This can only happen when you put your teammates first.

Imagine a server at a restaurant who is eating when customers arrive. Once the server sees the customer, he or she says, "As soon as I've wrapped up lunch, I'll be with you." In a short time, the restaurant would be out of business because the staff put themselves before the customer.

How does that translate to team captains? Many times it means they are the first ones to arrive at practice or a game and the last ones to leave after cleaning up. They choose to be last in line for a team dinner buffet, instead of insisting on being first. First there—last to leave.

You might be thinking, "Wait a minute, I do all the work behind the scenes and the team still goes in front of me? That's not right!" Of course, you can choose to go first and let everyone know you are the team captain, or you can humbly serve your team.

Serving beyond your team

Top-notch teams are willing serve their community as well. It's always inspiring for me to hear about high school athletic teams who are willing to volunteer a few hours to improve someone else's life.

When my son, DJ, was a team captain for football, he organized a community service project with the Feed My Starving Children organization. It was amazing to see 25 players willing to invest an afternoon of their time to pack meals for children in Third World countries. The experience of serving others and being selfless instead of selfish was a vital part of the team's pursuit of a season of significance.

Advanced Quality #2 Commitment

Each time a team captain is elected or selected, he or she must choose how to approach the vital role of leading the team. In my 25-plus years of experience presenting leadership workshops, three approaches to being a captain have become evident: Clueless, Casual, and Committed.

> "The only limit to your impact is your imagination and your commitment." -Tony Robbins

The Clueless Approach

A student–athlete taking the clueless approach doesn't take the role seriously. He or she may or may not even want the role. Typically, a team captain with the clueless approach is either very lazy or only wants to enjoy

Clueless Approach

the occasional glory the role sometimes provides. They like the fact their name is called during introductions, but when the team faces a difficult issue, clueless captains magically disappear. Clueless captains don't connect with their teammates, plan team-building events, or invest the time needed to learn leadership skills. It is unlikely that a clueless captain will help his or her team create a season of significance. They simply don't care enough about their role or the team.

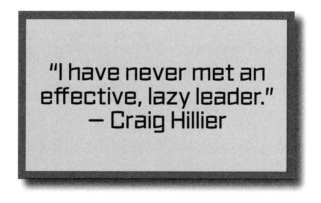

"I have never met an effective, lazy leader."
— Craig Hillier

The Casual Approach

The casual approach is typical of student–athletes who are interested in becoming a good leader. The casual team captain may put some extra effort into the role initially, but the

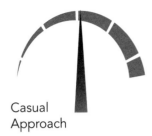

Casual
Approach

excitement of being named team captain fades quickly when the casual captain realizes how much work is required to be effective. Casual captains show flashes of effectiveness followed by flashes of doing very little to really lead the team. The casual approach does just enough to get by and usually flies under the radar. Casual leaders are more concerned about being "one of the gang" than they are about confronting a difficult issue that may be preventing the team from improving. Casual leaders will not be remembered as being strong, effective, and inspiring. Too often, this is the approach a majority of athletes take after being named team captain.

> Optional team functions are not optional for team captains—they are mandatory!

The Committed Approach

A student–athlete who takes the committed approach is dedicated 100% to the role of being a team captain. This young person understands it is an honor to serve as a team captain.

Committed Approach

The committed team captain goes out of his or her way to create team unity, work through conflict, and organize off-season practices and team bonding events.

The committed leader also understands that even at the high school level, he or she will learn important life lessons that will help them become successful in other areas of their life.

It's the committed leader who understands that "we" is more important than "me" and is willing to put in extra effort, which will often go unnoticed. Committed leaders have a strong desire to create a season of significance regardless of the team's overall record.

The committed captain realizes that the role has both benefits and challenges, but they know that the benefits of being committed will far outweigh anything that becomes a burden.

At this point, I hope you are asking yourself an important question: Am I going to take the committed approach to the upcoming athletic season? Or am I going to be clueless or casual?

Advanced Quality #3 Courage

Team captains will be called upon to handle difficult situations. At times it will take courage to confront a teammate who made a poor decision. While it may be tempting to ignore a challenging situation, strong team captains are willing to face the problem head on, even if it means a teammate may temporarily be upset to be called out.

The following "sticky situations" are all real. A sticky situation is a circumstance that arises and the decision of what to do isn't clear. Usually there are many options, and typically there isn't one right way and one wrong way.

Take a few moments and read through each of these sticky situations. Think about how you would respond if you were faced with the same set of circumstances.

1. *Sticky attitude situation*—A teammate constantly has a bad attitude. Everything is a major pain in the neck for this individual. When something goes wrong, she complains to anyone who will listen. Unfortunately, others listen, and her attitude is rubbing off on the team. What do you do?

2. *Sticky temper situation*—A key player has a short temper. His hot head has resulted in unsportsmanlike penalties several times. His temper and actions seem to rattle the team and coaches. What do you do?

3. *Sticky theft situation*—While competing in another town, one of your teammates steals a wallet or purse from the locker room. You appear to be the only one who witnesses the theft. What do you do?

4. *Sticky rival situation*—You just lost a close competition to your biggest rival. As you shake hands, players on the opposing team verbally rub it in that they won. What do you do?

5. *Sticky social situation*—One of your teammates seems more interested in the social part of being on the team than committing to having a great season. What do you do?

6. *Sticky coach situation*—Your coach becomes completely unglued and loses her temper after a loss. She uses foul language in a dramatic way. The coach berates almost every member of the team. What do you do? What is the best approach? If you choose to talk about the situation, to whom do you talk and when?

Advanced Quality #4 Camaraderie Builder

When I ask students why they participate in athletics, the number one thing that they say is, "It's fun." Most teens tell me that if it's not fun, they don't want to be involved.

Is it always going to be fun? Of course not. There are several things you have to experience that are not a lot of fun. The first two weeks of conditioning are not fun. Having teammates complain about everything under the sun is not fun. Practicing in extreme conditions is not fun. Despite these challenges, you should be enjoying your sport at least 80% of the time. It's common for students to start playing a sport at age five and burn out at 15 because every waking hour was spent either practicing or playing the sport. I'm all for working hard to be the best you can be. However, it's much easier to work hard when a team has created a strong camaraderie with each other. As my friend Keith Nord says, "There is nothing more fun than working hard for a goal."

To increase the camaraderie among your teammates, look for ways teammates can get to know each other and enjoy being with each other. Creating fun events and traditions on and off the court can develop camaraderie.

My high school football team had one tradition that is still with me today. It was called "The Pit." We played in an old stone stadium that was built in the 1940s. There was a small room built into the stadium with a dirt floor. It had a musty smell because of little air circulation. When the door was shut, it was pitch dark.

Every Thursday after practice, our entire team piled into The Pit. After everyone was in, the head coach walked in and shut the door behind him. No one could see a thing, and the only thing you could hear was people breathing. After five minutes of complete silence, the coach told a motivational story. After his story, he opened the floor up to the team captains and then to any person in the room to say whatever was on their heart. The code was "Whatever is said in The Pit, stays in The Pit."

I can't tell you specifics of what was said, but I can tell you that guys poured their hearts out. They said how much it meant to them to be a part of this team. They complimented the work ethic of specific individuals. Some teammates had powerful stories of their own to share. Throughout the week, we looked forward to Thursday's practice, because we knew we were going into The Pit.

Whenever I speak of or write about The Pit, I get goose bumps. When our class gets together for reunions, we spend at least an hour talking about the power of The Pit. Years later, it is still with each member of the team. So, what will your team do this year to create camaraderie?

Can you implement fun contests at the end of practice? Is there a drill or song you can do or sing after practice? Could you do an activity or play a different sport for fifteen minutes? Maybe a quick game of kickball is in order. How about showing up to cheer for another team from your school?

By showing up for other people's games, you're creating camaraderie with your team, while also creating school spirit. When this happens, other teams will often do the same for you. Make sure you're  having fun and planning fun events for the team.

Advanced Quality #5 Organization

"What time does the bus leave?" "Can I still order a T-shirt?" "What's the deadline to hand in the money from the fundraiser?" Team captains must be prepared to answer a lot of questions. They may also make contact with vendors like T-shirt printers, food suppliers, and fundraising companies.

It's impossible to stay on top of the details of being a team captain without effective organization. A phone and computer can be major tools to help you get and stay organized. There are several apps that allow you to store data on the cloud so they can be accessed by other team captains and coaches if necessary. Furthermore, cloud backup is vital if a laptop computer or phone gets lost, stolen, or damaged.

In addition to using an organization app, it will be helpful to create a "Captain's Kit." A simple three ring binder with a clear sleeve on the cover will work well.

The clear sleeve allows you to insert a team photo. Some team captains create a page with motivational phrases or the theme of the year to place in the sleeve. Purchasing divider tabs makes finding information easier as well. A Captain's Kit can be customized to suit your needs. You also need to print a calendar and add any of the following events that pertain to your sport.

Calendar

- ▶ Practice times

- ▶ Game schedule

- ▶ Bus departure times

- ▶ Captain's practices

- ▶ Fundraiser dates

- ▶ Date of photographs for team poster

A contact directory will allow you to quickly contact a player, parent, coach, or vendor via phone or email. Ideally, you have mailing addresses as well. It would also be beneficial to create a form for each type of contact. You can easily create a template using spreadsheet software such as Excel. This may sound "old school," but it will be very beneficial if something unfortunate happens to your phone or computer.

Contact Directory

- Coaches

- Teammates

- Teammates' parents/guardians—keep in mind family dynamics can be very diverse. You may need contact information for stepparents, guardians, grandparents, partners, etc. It is important to be respectful and sensitive to the variety of today's families.

- Vendors

Goals

- Team

- Personal

Article or Quotes

If you read an interesting article that would benefit your teammates, it's helpful to have easy access to it by placing it in your Captain's Kit. Creating a stockpile of motivational quotes will also be beneficial. You never know when your team will need a few words of inspiration before a practice or game.

Notes

You never know when an important thought will hit your mind. The notes section will become an area to "think out loud." And, many coaches ask their players to bring a notebook when reviewing film.

Thank You Notes with stamps

Top-notch captains send hand-written thank you notes to show appreciation. While it would be easier to send a text or email to the deserving party, a hand-written note indicates you took the time to write out your thoughts. You can purchase pre-printed notes or create your  own using your team or school logo. Remember to have stamps in your captain's kit so the note actually gets into the mail. An unsent or late thank you note is like running a race and stopping a foot before the finish line.

Have you ever received a note of appreciation six months after an event? This approach doesn't show very much class and is rather distasteful. The sooner you can send the thank you note, the more it shows you are an organized, class act.

Feel free to add additional content to your kit. If you take the time to design a Captain's Kit, you will avoid wasting time searching for information that could be accessed quickly. You will also create the impression with others that you have your act together instead of looking like an unorganized fool.

Advanced Quality #6 Communication

Have you ever been around someone who has a way with words? They know just the right thing to say or have the exact phrase to characterize a situation. It's remarkable how word power makes a difference in communication.

I have always been impressed with people who can articulate their thoughts in a way that catches the listener's ear. Leaders pay attention to specific words and phrases and specifically avoid words or phrases that may conjure negative feelings.

By making subtle shifts from standard language to *Leader's Language*, communication improves. Some people may ask, "Aren't you just playing with words?" The answer is, "Of course!" Leaders actually do play with words because using the right words in the right combination with the right tone and correct body language can make the difference between gaining agreement or causing dissention.

> "Think twice before you speak, because your words and influence will plant the seed of either success or failure in the mind of another." — Napoleon Hill

Try implementing *Leader's Language*, and you will be amazed with the improved connection you'll have with others. Consider these subtle shifts and why they matter:

Standard Language to *Leader's Language*

Change to *Adjust/Tweak*
Most people hate change. Yet the words "adjust" and "tweak" suggest a small shift rather than a massive conversion.

Have to *Get to*
When you "get to" do something, you no longer "have to" do anything. Remember, you "get to" go to practice and participate in sports. Even if you feel you have to, replace it with "get to" and you will feel different immediately.

Confusion to *Clarity*

If you don't understand something, it's vital to get clarity from a friend, teammate, or coach. Confusion suggests you don't get it or weren't focused when the message or instructions were given. Asking for clarity implies you have a basic understanding, but need more information.

"Me" to "We"

Regardless of your sport, it's vital to create a spirit of "we" instead of "me." When someone asks a team leader or captain, "How is your season going?" It's much better to say, "We are doing well" instead of "I'm doing well." Discuss or mention points that the entire team is accomplishing or working on.

Boast to *Blessed*

Too often athletes are bragging or boasting about team or personal statistics. People are drawn to others who feel blessed with their achievements and how the season is progressing.

Can't to *Up until now*

The word "can't" builds a mental wall that prevents people from becoming their best. By stating, "up until now," we/I haven't been able to achieve the goal," it implies you are still pursuing the goal.

Problem to *Opportunity*

Most of us hate problems, but we look forward to opportunities. For example, a school may have a problem with school spirit or they may have an opportunity to improve school spirit by engaging their student leaders.

To be honest with you to *Let me be straightforward*
When someone says to me, "to be honest with you..."
I usually think, "So you haven't been honest with me up
until now?" Leaders may have difficult conversations with
teammates or coaches. It's possible you'll have to say
some difficult words that may not go over well. By using
the phrase "let me be straightforward" means you are
sharing what you really think without sugar coating it.

At first glance these changes may seem minuscule. But
implementing the subtle shift from standard language to
the *Leader's Language* will transform your communication
effectiveness.

Shifting into the role of team captain is a progression and
doesn't happen instantly. Adopting all six advanced qualities will take a considerable amount of time. That's why
they are considered advanced qualities. It would be wise
to let the content in this chapter soak in before advancing
to the next chapter. You might even re-read the chapter in
a few days so that you have
a stronger understanding of
how to shift from team leader
to team captain.

The next chapter shifts to
cultivating a strong working
relationship with your coach
and coaching staff.

Please go to the **Certification Packet** in section three to
complete the application exercises for this chapter.

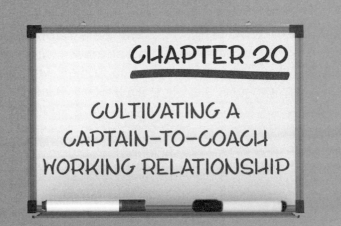

CHAPTER 20

CULTIVATING A CAPTAIN-TO-COACH WORKING RELATIONSHIP

"Agreements prevent disagreements." —Harvey McKay

As a child, my brother, sister, and I would often spend a week in the summer with both sets of grandparents; they were farmers. Living on a farm is a stark contrast from living in town. The best part of the week was riding in the tractor cab with either grandpa. I recall my grandpa saying, "Let's use the cultivator on the corn." As we were walking to the tractor, I asked my grandpa, "What does a cultivator do?" He said, "It's a tool that attaches to the tractor that has several metal points that go in the ground. Cultivating opens the earth between rows of corn." I asked, "Why do you need to do that?" He said, "Loosening the soil helps the corn grow and doesn't let the weeds grow."

After cultivating for a few hours, we had to refuel the tractor. As the gas was being pumped into the tractor, I asked grandpa, "This takes a long time, huh, Grandpa?" He said, "It does take a lot of time, and gas is expensive. But if you don't do it, the weeds take over and can strangle your crop. The time spent doing this now will benefit the crop later."

Some time after, I learned that the first round of cultivating took place when the corn was just a few inches tall. Shields would be placed over the steel cutting points to insure the cultivator would not damage the new, vulnerable corn plants. A farmer had to move slowly and carefully, because the sharp metal points could destroy the plants. The last round of cultivating happened when the corn was a few feet tall. Because the roots were stronger, the shields were removed, and a farmer could move much faster through the planted rows.

Coaches and team captains must cultivate a working relationship to have a season of significance. Think back to what my grandpa said: "If you don't take the time to cultivate, the weeds take over and strangle your crop." Maybe you have been part of a team where the weeds were not controlled, and soon they ruled the field.

By cultivating or discussing the following points prior to the season, your team will develop and grow, and the weeds or distractions won't strangle the season.

> "If we don't take time to cultivate, the weeds take over and strangle your crop."
>
> — Grandpa Hillier

Ideally, schedule a meeting several months before the season begins and bring this book with you to the meeting. This approach shows the coach you are serious about becoming a great leader by reading about, reflecting on, and applying proven leadership strategies. Having the book in your hand will also help guide an important, but potentially awkward, conversation. Finally, by writing down the answers to the questions on the Captain-To-Coach Questionnaire in the Certification Packet, you'll have a quick reference to the key points from the meeting.

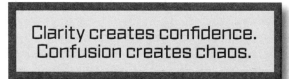

> ## Clarity creates confidence.
> ## Confusion creates chaos.

Thousands of captains have used the Captain-to-Coach Questionnaire to gain insight into their role. Remember, coaches view their captains in a variety of ways. Some coaches see captains as an extension of the coaching staff, whereas other coaches place little importance on captains. The questionnaire features several pointed questions that will unearth some very important information about your specific roles and responsibilities for the season. In essence, the Captain-to-Coach Questionnaire will become the playbook for how you will work together throughout your time as a team captain.

Pointed Question #1: "What do you expect from me this season?"

Frustrations occur when one person has unmet expectations with another person. Too often, these expectations have never been communicated. Your goal is to get a clear definition of what your coach wants from you.

 Pointed Question #2: "If you were to write a job description for me this season, what would it say?"

Chances are this is your first experience as a team captain. You are looking for specific responses in this question. A job description should describe what the coach expects from you every day as well as what's expected of you for the overall season.

Pointed Question #3: "How can I help you this season?"

Team captains rarely ask this question, so you'll stand out when you do. Usually, captains focus on what the coach can do for them. Coaching is a difficult job. This question is designed to show the coach you're committed to a season of significance and that you're thinking of the team instead of just yourself.

Pointed Question #4: "What's the process to address problems and concerns this season?"

Every team deals with issues during the season. When these issues show their ugly heads, it's key to have a plan of attack. Average teams and team captains just let things slide and hope these difficulties go away. Captains and teams who are willing to have a difficult discussion on an uncomfortable topic create the opportunity to solve the issue and move forward. This question will outline the range of discussions a coach desires from a team captain.

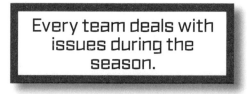

> Every team deals with issues during the season.

Assume a player has a problem or concern with the coach. Some coaches ask the captain to bring the concern to the coach during a meeting. Other coaches encourage the captain to ask the player to approach the coach directly. **The key is to define the process.** As a team captain, you must know the process to which you and your coach will commit when working through difficult times.

Pointed Question #5: "What do I need to understand that I may not know now?"

This should generate an interesting response from your coach. The response may be simple or complex. It will certainly provide a piece of information you wouldn't have gathered without asking the question. Keep in mind that if your coach gives feedback for personal areas of improvement, a strong team captain will listen and absorb the information without becoming heated or defensive.

Pointed Question #6: "How will our personality styles mesh this year?"

Ideally, your coach completed the **T.E.A.M. Dynamics Personality Indicator** featured in Chapter 5. This would be a great opportunity to discuss your leading role, supporting role, and villain role and compare them to your coach's roles. It would also be wise to review the descriptions of each style and have a candid discussion on how the styles compare and contrast.

By understanding how each style works, a coach and captain can create a stronger working relationship, because the personality indicator sheds incredible light on how each style operates.

The Power of Understanding Each Other's Personality Style

After presenting a leadership workshop, a team captain approached me and said, "The T.E.A.M. Dynamics Personality Indicator was life changing." His leading role was Togetherness and his villain role was Enterpriser. The young man went on to say, "After learning about each style, I know my coach is an Enterpriser. I have had a hard time playing for him, because he is always in my face. He is always yelling at me and never says anything positive, even when I do everything right. I decided this morning before the conference I wasn't going to play this year. After hearing about the differences we have, I have decided not to quit. I'm going to go through this questionnaire with him and have him take the T.E.A.M. Dynamics pro ile and show him my results too. I think we can igure out a way to work together now. Thanks for doing the conference. I wouldn't have played this year without this information, and I know I would have regretted it for a long time."

I will never forget that conversation. Because he was unaware of the 6 pointed questions to cover prior to the season, and didn't understand how different personalities functioned, a young man nearly missed out on participating his senior year.

It would be a huge mistake to ignore this questionnaire and proceed into a sports season without a clear discussion of your role as team captain. Again, it's impossible to create a universal checklist of responsibilities for team captains, because every sport is unique. By taking the time to have your coach clarify what he/she is expecting, you can be more con ident in your role.

The Captain-to-Coach Questionnaire is a great starting place for establishing a strong working relationship with your coach. But one pre-season conversation doesn't provide enough time, information, or discussion to form a working relationship that will endure throughout the season. And, having sporadic, short meetings is rarely effective. Ideally, a coach sets up a series of meetings in the off-season as well as during the season that will cover several objectives, which could include:

- Reviewing and applying leadership lessons from a variety of resources including this book, videos, articles, other leadership books, newspaper articles, and so on. Normally, this type of content is emphasized more in pre-season meetings than during in-season meetings.

- Getting an update on the vibe of the team and the season.

- Discussing the goals, objectives, and plans for upcoming practices and competitions.

- Talking about issues that are happening either inside or outside the sport or season.

Developing and cultivating a strong working relationship with your coach must be done on a consistent basis. A farmer would not plant seeds in the spring and ignore the crop until the fall by neglecting to cultivate it periodically.

A captain and coach must cultivate their working relationship throughout the season. When both parties are willing to unearth the dirt to enhance a team's growth and keep the weeds from strangling the season, everyone will look back at the year with fondness. Coaches and players understand a team's win–loss is important, but the relationships that are created along the way will last much longer than any high school athletic season.

The **Certification Packet** in section 3 includes the Captain-to-Coach Questionnaire along with additional review and application exercises.

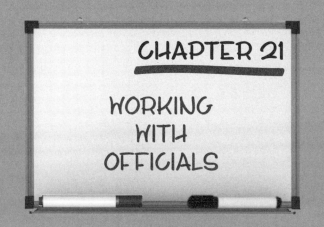

CHAPTER 21

WORKING WITH OFFICIALS

"The trouble with referees is that they just don't care which side wins." —Tom Canterbury

When interviewing officials for this book, I discovered several insightful suggestions about sportsmanship and how to work effectively with officials. I think you will find this information important and useful throughout the season. Even if your sport does not interact with officials, you will gain some leadership tips from this chapter.

First Impressions are Important

Depending on your sport, you may meet with officials prior to the game. The way you conduct yourself creates an impression on the officials. It's important to take a pregame meeting with officials seriously. As you approach an official, look him or her in the  eye and introduce yourself. At some sporting events, the atmosphere can be very loud prior to game time. You may have to adjust your voice so the official can hear your name. Many times a handshake takes place between the officials and the other team captains. The best handshakes are firm but not overpowering. Make sure to get each officials' name during the introduction as well. Later on, if you need to speak with them, address them as Mr. or Ms. "Referee/Official" (last name). It's best to avoid calling them by their first name, as this is too casual. It's better to be formal and have an official say, "Please call me Ben/Beth" than to address them by their first name and have them say, "It's Ms. Johnson." The last thing you want to do is create a poor impression by being too casual.

Each venue based on the sport is different. If there is something unique or special about the venue, the time to get clarification is during the pregame meeting. For example, sometimes gymnasium  floors have so many lines it's difficult to recognize which ones are for your particular sport. If you have a venue question, the pregame meeting is the perfect time to ask your questions.

Mistakes can happen

No one is perfect. That includes officials. They're going to make mistakes from time to time. Their goal is to call a game or match in a fair, consistent manner. Normally, they are officiating because they enjoy working with teens and still want to be a part of a sport. If you are expecting them to call a perfect game, you're setting yourself up for disappointment.

Officials admit they are going to miss a call. Sometimes those calls will be in your favor, sometimes they won't. It usually balances out in the end. Keep the mistakes in

A perfect game has never been played or perfectly officiated

perspective and control the things you can control. One official said, **"A perfect game has never been played or perfectly officiated."**

Be Respectful

It's important to watch your attitude and behavior toward officials. I asked several officials, "If a team has an arrogant attitude and is disrespectful, does that play a role in how you call the game or match?" Every official I interviewed said basically the same thing, "It shouldn't, but it could." In other words, your personal conduct and attitude could play a role in how the officials see the game. Why take a chance on this when you can make a positive impact from the beginning?

I was watching my son play on a traveling baseball team. It was an away game. The umpire appeared to be in his early twenties. Our team was leading by two runs and one of our players hit a powerful, long ball close to the home run fence. The left fielder was sprinting back toward the fence. He stretched out to catch the ball briefly, but his momentum took him face first into the chain-link fence. He dropped the ball and lay there. The center fielder raced over to grab the ball and throw it to the infield. It was almost an ESPN catch that turned into a triple for our team. One player on our team, known to have a loud mouth, shouted, "Did you see that idiot drop the ball?"

The next thing we know the umpire takes off his mask and walks toward our dugout. He yelled, "I'm not sure which kid just made that comment, but it was out of line. Whoever said it owes that kid an apology. It was just about a great catch."

It was easy to see the ump's feelings based on the redness in his face. He was ticked off at the situation and our team. For the rest of the game, we saw the strike zone become larger for our opponent and smaller when we were on the mound.

It's rather uncommon to see an official directly confront a team in anger like the umpire in the story. However, while they may not say anything out loud, the baseball incident proves that officials are watching and listening. Because they are human, it's very possible that disrespectful crowds, coaches, and players can play a small role in how the game is officiated.

Watch your mouth

Officials grow tired of players questioning every call or letting out a loud sigh after a call has been made. It's best to just keep quiet after a call even if you disagree with it. If someone needs to question a call, it's best if a coach does it.

A good friend of mine officiates several sports. Despite years of experience, players and coaches often scream and disagree with his calls. With one simple, magical, phrase, he instantly diffuses the situation. Mr. Erickson simply says, "Talk to me like you'd like me to talk to you." Think about that powerful statement for a minute. If a coach or player continues to rant and rave, he repeats the phrase and says, "I'll be back and listen when you are ready to **'Talk to me like you'd like me to talk to you.'**" This phrase can be used in all kinds of situations where someone is using an angry or disrespectful tone.

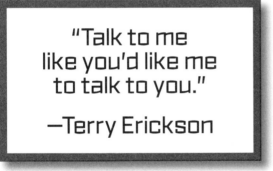

> # "Talk to me like you'd like me to talk to you."
> ## —Terry Erickson

I remember the first time I used the phrase with my daughter, who was in 8th grade at the time. My wife had back-to-back evening school conferences and had not had time to make the weekly grocery store run. No more than ten seconds after I walked through the door having finished a four-day speaking tour, she started in with me. "Dad, it's about time you got home. We have no food in the house. (*No food she liked.*) We are out of yo-gurt, bananas, and chicken. How come we don't have any food?" I was not thrilled with her tone of voice, because I was exhausted from the trip. It would have been easy to match her tone and say, "I've been gone for four days, and I have no idea what's in the refrigerator." Of course, this would not have helped the situation much.

I simply said, "Talk to me like you'd like me to talk to you." At first this didn't register and her tone was the same. The second time I repeated the phrase, it connected with her and her approach changed, "Dad, we are out of food I like." I replied, "Let's hop in the car and go to the store then."

She said, "Ok, that's what I wanted to do when you got home." I had to smile and laugh as I thought to myself, had she approached it with the right tone to begin with, we could have been on our way to the store a while ago and enjoyed catching up with each other.

Know the rules

If you truly understand the rules of the game, you will have a lot more credibility with the officials. If you ask them an uninformed question, they may start to wonder how much you really understand your sport. Get the rulebook and take time to go through it.

Know when and how to ask questions during competition

The officials I interviewed gave me several key pointers on asking questions. The first one is to know the difference between a judgment call and a rule interpretation call.

A judgment call could include unsportsmanlike conduct, an offensive charge in basketball, or whether gymnastic leaps were at a medium or superior level. You will have little or no success in convincing an official to change this type of call. You may learn something by asking how the official saw the event, but it's rare to see an official reverse a judgment call.

A rule interpretation is different. It could include why a receiver became ineligible to receive a pass after going out of bounds or why a base runner on first is automatically out if the ball is popped to an infielder. If an official makes a mistake on a rule interpretation call, there is a chance the call may be reversed. The key is to fully understand the rule. If you feel confident in your knowledge on a rule interpretation call, you may respectfully approach the official and ask for permission to ask them a question.

The best way to ask a question is to approach an official when he is not involved in another task. Ask, "Is it okay for me to ask you a question?" Make sure your tone of voice is positive. Remember: Talk to me like you'd like me to talk to you.

If it's an appropriate time, the official will usually allow you to ask the question. Then you might say something such as, "I thought the rule was..." and then state your case. The official will explain his reasoning behind the call. If the official was wrong, he could correct the decision. Typically, a call won't be reversed, but the official's explanation will tell you something about how he will be officiating the rest of the contest.

Every official is different. One set of officials may be strict with the rules, whereas others may just let you play. The best teams adjust and play their hearts out regardless of the officiating.

Officiate a youth league competition

One of the best suggestions officials gave me about helping high school athletes learn more about working with them is to officiate in a youth league. It's a surefire way to see what officials go through. You will have an opportunity to hear the moans and groans from the crowd and watch the players react to your calls.

A famous NFL television commentator was known to be critical of officials during his broadcasts. He was invited to take part in the officials' boot camp. He figured he would probably teach the officials a thing or two.

Needless to say, this experience completely changed him. He was amazed at how difficult it was to be in the middle of the action and try to call a fair game. Now when he's in the broadcasting booth, his comments on officiating are different. He is more supportive of officials' calls even when the instant replay showed that the official made a mistake. Take an opportunity to be an "unofficial" official, and see what you can learn. I promise it will be an eye-opening experience.

How you conduct yourself when working with officials says a lot about you and your team. Make sure you are aware of the challenges of officiating an athletic contest. Part of your legacy as a team captain will be determined by your interactions with officials. The final chapter in the book will challenge you to think about what your legacy will be after high school is complete and your playing days are behind you.

Please go to the **Certification Packet** in section three to complete the application exercises for this chapter.

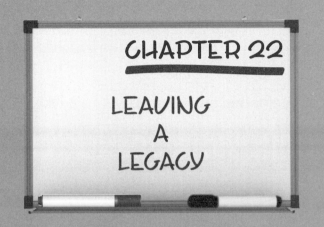

CHAPTER 22

LEAVING A LEGACY

"Carve your name on hearts, not tombstones. A legacy is etched into the minds of others and the stories they share about you." –Shannon L. Alder

One of my favorite questions to ask an audience during a workshop is, *"Think back to being a freshman or sophomore and tell me about a team leader or captain you admired. Share why you admired them."*

The responses are very inspiring. Almost all of the stories revolve around a team captain who was willing to go out of his or her way to make everyone feel included: Younger athletes, teammates who rarely played, or a team star felt as if they were truly an important part of the team.

I remember a young woman shared a story about how her team captain drove to her house to pick her up for off-season training in cross country. Another young man, a freshman, described how a senior team captain stayed after wrestling practice to help him improve his escapes. Many students have described team captains who simply had a great attitude that made practice and games fun.

Sadly, when this question is asked of 150 student athletes in a workshop, only a handful of students have an example to share with the group. This response indicates only a small percentage of team captains have left a legacy.

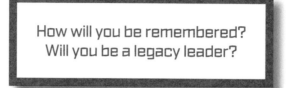

How will you be remembered?
Will you be a legacy leader?

If you have read this far into the book, you have proven you want to be the best team leader and captain as possible. If your peers or underclassmen were asked five years after high school graduation to describe a legendary student leader, would your name be a part of the conversation?

If your response is, "I don't really care," you will not be an effective captain! If you hear the question and think, "I'm going to do everything possible to leave a positive legacy," chances are strong your name will be brought up when others are asked to name a legendary leader.

Becoming a legendary leader does not happen by accident. It takes tremendous effort to become a leader who is remembered long after graduating from high school.

"My legacy is that I stayed on course
from the beginning to the end,
because I believed
in something inside of me."
— Tina Turner

By applying the ideas, tools, and strategies in this book, you can become the captain younger athletes aspire to be if they are selected to represent their team as a captain in the future. Remember, being a team captain is an honor. The opportunity to be fired up and lead your team to a season of significance is in front of you. What are you going to do?

What are you going to do?

The opportunity is in front of you.
What are you going to do?

Leadership is *not* for everyone.
It's *not* about being better than anyone else.
It's *not* about the * next to your name in a program.
It's *not* about glory.
It's *not* about having your name called out in a special fashion for introductions.
It's *not* about being in the front of a team poster.

It's *not* about you!

It *is* about helping others get better.
It *is* about dealing with uncomfortable situations.
It *is* about staying organized in a chaotic world.
It *is* about being the hardest worker on the team.
It *is* about bringing it every day.
It *is* about taking your team on a journey to a season of significance. . .regardless of your record.

Your coaches can't do it for you.
Your parents can't do it for you.

The opportunity is in front of you.
What are you going to do?

It's not going to be easy.
There will be bumps in the road.
You will meet obstacles along the way.
People won't always like you.
Teammates will want you to give them a break.
Coaches will be in your face.
Sometimes you will wonder why you wanted to take on a leadership role.
But, at the end of the day the payoff is huge.
Because you stepped up and committed to being all in instead of all out.
The season was significant because of your leadership.

So, the opportunity is in front of you.
What are you going to do?

Please go to the **Certification Packet** in section three to complete the application exercises for this chapter.

Extra Steps Section

Contents

All pages in the Extra Steps section
are perforated for easy removal.

CERTIFICATION PACKET OVERVIEW

"Knowledge is not power—Action is power!"
—Tony Robbins

This packet is designed to help you take action on the ideas and strategies shared in the book. Through a variety of review exercises, you will be able to incorporate the content into your leadership journey.

*As a reminder, the **Team Leader** section consists of Chapters 1 through 18. **The Team Captain** section runs from Chapter 19 through 22.*

> This Certification Packet is flexible and can be customized to meet a variety of needs.

Because everyone can benefit from reading the book, it's common for coaches to have an entire team read it and complete various pages from the packet. Some coaches assign the entire team leader section, whereas other coaches create a customized approach for various members of the team.

Many coaches ask identified team leaders and potential team leaders to complete the packet through the team leader section.

Numerous athletic directors and coaches use a structured application process to select team captains. Athletes who participate in this process complete a variety of tasks prior to being named a team captain. In this case, the entire Certification Packet might be assigned. After the assigned tasks and Certification Packet have been reviewed by a coach or the AD, an athlete can move to the next step in their given process.

Your responses to the variety of review exercises allow a coach or athletic director to:

- Learn more about you
- Provide a platform for further discussion on leadership topics covered in the book
- Gauge your commitment to leadership based on the depth of your answers
- Verify you have a strong understanding of leadership, thus providing confidence as a team leader or captain

Too often, people proceed through a book without taking the time to reflect and apply how they can use the content. It's important to take enough time to complete the exercises for each chapter thoroughly.

The certification packet will become a major tool and resource for you as you embark on a season of significance. Whether the certification packet is required, or simply an independent learning tool, great leaders will take the time and effort to proceed through the Certification Packet.

Recommendation:

Most students find it is best to leave the **Certification Packet** in the book until it is finished. After you have completed the assigned pages, carefully remove the pages a few at a time.

Warning: Attempting to remove the entire packet at once will likely cause the pages to tear.

HIGH SCHOOL
sports leader

Certification Packet

Coaching Team Leaders and Captains to a Season of Significance!

Name _____

Opening Chapter: Creating a Season of Signficance

In the *Realizing a Need* opening chapter, Craig outlines his leadership story as a high school leader and a team captain. It will be valuable to reflect on your thoughts regarding leadership. Take a few minutes to review the following questions and then write your answer on the lines. The key in any self-evaluation survey is to be 100% honest with your responses. Answering these questions will create a baseline regarding your journey into leadership.

Complete the following phrase from the opening chapter. Leadership is a _____ —not _____ .

In your opinion, why is this phrase important to understand?

_____

_____

_____

A quote in the opening chapter read, "There are some team leaders who are not team captains, and there are some team captains who are not team leaders." What are your thoughts on this statement? _____

_____

_____

Do you consider yourself a leader now? Why or why not?

_____

_____

_____

Describe some of the experiences you have had with leadership. _____

_____

_____

In your opinion, why would someone willingly follow you as a leader? _____

_____

_____

_____

Significance is defined as "meaningful, important, and memorable."

Students from Craig's live workshops generated a list of the top 10 things that can prevent a season of significance. Think about your upcoming athletic season. Rank the list, randomly created, from 1 to 10 for your team, where 1 is the thing you are most concerned about and 10 is the item you are least concerned about.

_____ Selfishness
_____ Little or no talent
_____ Issues with the coach
_____ Bad decisions outside the sport that create drama
_____ Poor or no leadership
_____ Complaining teammates
_____ Infractions
_____ Lack of preparation
_____ Injuries
_____ Poor attitude

Write your top three concerns about your ability to create a season of significance:

    1. _____
    2. _____
    3. _____

What can be done to address these issues?

_____

_____

_____

_____

Chapter 1: Practicing the Fundamentals

Complete the statement. If you are_____fundamentally _____—you_____ _____.

The opening of the story covered how pride affects learning. Describe a time when you let personal pride get in the way of learning. _____

_____

_____

_____

Specifically, what lessons did you take from Chapter 1?

_____

_____

_____

How can you apply the above lessons in life and in sports?

_____

_____

_____

Check any of the boxes that apply to your motivation for reading this book.

☐   I'm excited to learn more about leadership.

☐   I'm optimistic because it could help me and my team have a great season.

☐   I'm willing to read it, but not necessarily excited about it.

☐   I'm going to proceed because I'm supposed to.

☐   I'm not going to put much effort into this, as it will be a waste of time.

Chapter 2: Embracing the Seasons of Leadership

Write the seasons of leadership so they are in sequential order.

Refining   1. _____

Empowering   2. _____

Awakening   3. _____

Strengthening   4. _____

Keeping your current age and sports level in mind, (varsity, junior varsity, etc.), what season of leadership do you see yourself in right now? Why?

_____

_____

_____

_____

_____

In your opinion, what's great about the *Awakening* season?

_____

_____

_____

In your opinion, what's great about the *Strengthening* season?

_____

_____

_____

_____

_____

In your opinion, what's difficult about being in the *Refining* season?

_____

_____

_____

_____

_____

As noted, only a small percentage of people enter the *Empowering* season. In your opinion, why is this the case? _____

_____

_____

_____

_____

_____

Have you ever felt as if you were in the Empowering season? If so, describe what you experienced. If not, what obstacles did you encounter to being empowering?

_____

_____

_____

_____

_____

_____

_____

_____

Chapter 3: Emerging as a Leader

It's now time for you to gauge yourself on the top ten qualities of team leaders. Each quality has a line gauge. You will assess yourself on a spectrum from:

← ─────────────────────────────── →
Rarely Occasionally Usually Consistently

The only way for this exercise to work is to be 100% honest with yourself. I have never met anyone who could legitimately be rated "consistently" on all ten qualities. So, be candid when you assess yourself. The only way to improve as a leader is to be brutally honest about your strengths and areas for improvement.

In thinking about each quality, ask yourself, "Realistically, how often do I demonstrate this quality?" Remember to examine your actions—not your intentions. Often, we intend to show a quality, but we may not act on the intention. *Others see our actions, not our intentions.* Simply place an X on the line where you see yourself on each of the qualities covered in chapter 3. Once you have completed the task, answer the reflection questions.

Rarely Occasionally Usually Consistently

← ─────────────────────────────── →
Trust

← ─────────────────────────────── →
Passion

← ─────────────────────────────── →
Strong Work Ethic

← ─────────────────────────────── →
Resilience

← ─────────────────────────────── →
Integrity

← ─────────────────────────────── →
Coachability

← ─────────────────────────────── →
Flexibility

← ─────────────────────────────── →
Accountable

← ─────────────────────────────── →
Confidence

← ─────────────────────────────── →
Caring

CQ stands for C _____ Q _____

Based on the gauges, which two are your greatest strengths?

1. _____

2. _____

As you read, it is very rare for any leader to be consistent on all 10 qualities. Based on the gauges, which two qualities could you improve?

1. _____

2. _____

How can you improve on the two qualities listed above? Be specific. (*It's important to be detailed in your response. For example, if strong work ethic needs improvement, simply writing, "Work Harder," is too vague for an action plan. The more specific you are, the better the odds of implementing the action plan.*)

_____

_____

_____

_____

_____

The chapter covered the top 10 qualities of team leaders based on research from student surveys. In your opinion, name two qualities that could be added to the list and share their importance.

1. _____

_____

2. _____

_____

Chapter 4: Creating Team Chemistry

Team chemistry is created and measured by balancing
_____ and _____

Five stages of teamwork are outlined in Chapter 4. Using
the numbers 1 through 5, arrange the order of the stages.

_____Storm _____Form_____ Reform_____Norm_____Perform

The *storm* stage is pivotal for creating team chemistry.
Describe a situation where you, or a team on which you
played, experienced a *healthy* storm. Detail the outcome
of the experience.

_____

_____

_____

_____

Describe a situation where you, or a team on which you
played, experienced a *toxic* storm. Detail the outcome of
the experience.

_____

_____

_____

_____

_____

_____

_____

_____

_____

_____

In your opinion, what are the keys to a team storm that is healthy?

_____

_____

_____

_____

The *reform* stage of teamwork is a constant. Describe a situation where you, or a team on which you played, had to reform on the spot.

_____

_____

_____

_____

_____

_____

Chapters 5 through 10: T.E.A.M. Dynamics Personality Indicator

The T.E.A.M. Dynamics Personality Indicator provides incredible insight into how four personality styles might affect how you approach life and leadership. It will be helpful to process how you can use and apply the content from the personality indicator. Understanding how to blend individual roles into team goals is a vital part of creating a season of significance.

Circle your Leading Role
Draw a check mark next to your √ Supporting Role
Draw an X next to your X Villain Role

Togetherness	Analyzer
Enterpriser	Motivator

Considering all three roles, in your opinion, what are the specific *advantages* of your leadership style?

_____

_____

_____

_____

Considering all three roles, in your opinion, what are the specific *disadvantages* of your leadership style?

_____

_____

_____

_____

Each style is featured in its own detailed chapter that outlines strategies for working with each of the other styles. For you, which style is typically difficult for you to work with and communicate?

_____

_____

_____

_____

What specific adjustments can you make to create a stronger connection to this style?

_____

_____

_____

_____

Which leadership style do you think is most characteristic of your head coach? (Circle his/her Leading Role)

Togetherness   Enterpriser   Analyzer   Motivator

Keeping your own style in mind, what are the specific strengths of combining your style and your coach's style?

_____

_____

_____

_____

_____

_____

What do you need to remember, adjust, or improve in order to be a stronger communicator with your coach?

_____

_____

_____

_____

_____

What was your biggest takeaway from the T.E.A.M. Dynamics Personality Indicator?

_____

_____

_____

_____

_____

In your opinion, why is it important to know and understand leadership styles?

_____

_____

_____

_____

_____

_____

_____

_____

_____

_____

_____

Chapter 11: Visualizing Results

Write out the GOALS formula using the first letter of each word: G_____ O_____

A_____ L_____ S_____

Each component in the GOALS formula is important. In your opinion, which component is most important for you as goals are established as a team or as an individual?

_____

_____

_____

In your opinion, how important is it to have goals established for all areas of your life? Why?

_____

_____

_____

Use the spaces below to set two goals. You can decide if they are individual or team goals. Write your goal so that if you showed it to someone you were meeting for the first time, he or she would know and understand what you are pursuing.

Chapter 12: Refusing Drugs and Alcohol

Using drugs and alcohol can interfere with a season of significance. Without naming specific individuals, under what circumstances have you seen the negative impact of alcohol and drugs on high school athletes?

_____

_____

_____

_____

_____

_____

_____

The chapter listed several detrimental aspects of using drugs and alcohol. In your opinion, what are the top three damaging effects? Explain either from an individual or team perspective.

_____

_____

_____

_____

_____

_____

As you read, you have the rest of your life to drink if you so choose. You only have one chance to be involved in high school athletics. On the following page is a student pledge to be drug and alcohol free. After reading the pledge, decide if you can commit to it. If you can, sign your name at the bottom. Ideally, this pledge will be presented and discussed in a team meeting. After everyone is familiar with the expectations, other athletes can commit to themselves, their teammates, coaches, and parents to being drug and alcohol free.

Student's Pledge

As an athlete, I agree to abide by all rules regarding the use of drugs. I understand that drug addiction is a disease and, even though it may be treatable, it has serious physical and emotional effects—effects that would hurt me, my family, my team, and my school. Given the serious dangers of drug use, I accept and pledge to follow all rules and laws established by my school, team, and community regarding the use of drugs. These include the rules listed in my school's student and athletic handbooks and any other rules established by my coach. To demonstrate my support, I pledge to:

1. Support my fellow students by setting an example and abstaining from the use of alcohol and illegal drugs.

2. Avoid enabling any of my fellow students or teammates who use these substances. I will not cover up or lie for them if any rules are broken. I will hold my fellow students and teammates fully responsible and accountable for their actions.

3. Seek information and assistance in dealing with my own or other students' problems relating to drugs and alcohol.

4. Be honest and open with my parents or guardians about my feelings and problems.

5. Be honest and open with my coach and other school or community personnel.

_____

Student   Date

** PARENTS OR GUARDIANS: We ask that you **co-sign this pledge to show your support.**

_____

Parent/Guardian   **Date**

_____

Parent/Guardian   **Date**

Reprinted with permission from The Coach's Playbook Against Drugs, published by the Office of Juvenile Justice and Delinquency Prevention (OJJDP), Washington, DC.

Chapter 13: Setting the Stage

List the five keys to setting the stage:
1. _____
2. _____
3. _____
4. _____
5. _____

Of all the leadership stories shared in chapter 13, which one was most important to you? Explain why.

_____
_____
_____
_____

Which of the five keys listed above do you already demonstrate on a consistent basis? Explain why.

_____
_____
_____

Which of the five keys listed above do you need to improve? Explain why.

_____
_____
_____

What was the most important thing you learned from this chapter? How can you apply it in your life or athletics?

_____
_____
_____

Chapter 14: Rebounding from a Loss or Poor performance

List the policies on rebounding from a loss or poor performance.

1. _____
2. _____
3. _____
4. _____
5. _____

No one likes to lose or perform poorly in athletics. Describe a time when you responded poorly to making a mistake or losing. What were the results?

_____
_____
_____

Leaders understand their response to a given situation can be have a domino effect with their teammates. Describe a situation when you witnessed a person or team rebound positively from a poor performance or loss. What did you learn from this experience? Please be specific.

_____
_____
_____

Of the five policies listed above, which one(s) are most helpful to you? Explain why.

_____
_____
_____
_____
_____

Chapter 15: Avoiding the Hazards of Hazing

Complete the following sentence. "In Chapter 15, hazing is defined as _____

_____

In your opinion, what are the potential costs of team hazing?

_____

_____

_____

_____

Research a hazing incident via a newspaper, magazine, or Internet article. Briefly outline the hazing incident along with the outcome or penalty.

_____

_____

_____

_____

What is one positive team bonding experience your team could institute this season?

_____

_____

_____

_____

Optional: If your team has a history of hazing, discuss with your teammates how this action could detract from your season of significance. Ideally, determine an action plan to eliminate it and replace it with the idea listed above or another positive activity.

_____

_____

_____

Chapter 16: Dealing with Conflict

"To get it right, you have to see it right."

What is your typical pattern for dealing with conflict? For example, do you withdraw and become silent? Verbally attack the other person or group? Deny there is an issue or joke about it? What results do you achieve using this pattern?

_____

_____

_____

Rate your comfort level regarding dealing with conflict by placing an X at the appropriate spot and explain why.

←————————————————————————————→

Very Comfortable   Comfortable   Very *Uncomfortable*

_____

_____

What is important when starting a conversation when there is a conflict? _____

_____

_____

_____

What do each one of the letters stand for in the OTFDN formula?

O _____

T _____

F _____

D _____

N _____

What is the most important take away from this chapter related to dealing with conflict? Explain why.

_____

_____

_____

Chapter 17: Managing Social Media

Which of the four opening stories had the most impact on you? Explain why. _____

_____

_____

In your opinion, what is great about social media?

_____

_____

_____

In your opinion, what concerns you about social media?

_____

_____

_____

What are the Four Fundamental Factors of Social Media?

➡️

➡️

➡️

➡️

What is the **POST** formula for social media?

P _____
O _____
S _____
T _____

How can you use social media in a positive way to create a season of significance?_____

_____

_____

_____

Chapter 18: Demonstrating C.L.A.S.S. through Sportsmanship

An important statement in Chapter 18 reads, "Sportsmanship boils down to _____ , accepting _____ and _____ to be a _____ regardless of the _____

Without naming an individual, describe an incident where a teammate or athlete demonstrated poor sportsmanship.

_____

_____

_____

_____

Research a story via a newspaper, magazine, or the Internet when an athlete demonstrated great sportsmanship. Describe the story and share your thoughts.

_____

_____

_____

_____

_____

What is the C.L.A.S.S. formula?

C _____

L _____

A _____

S _____

S _____

As a high school leader, describe a few specific ways you can demonstrate sportsmanship in your sports team.

_____

_____

_____

_____

As a high school leader, describe a few specific ways you can demonstrate sportsmanship beyond your sport. Example situations might include the classroom, school hallways, being a spectator for another high school sport, and so on._____

_____

_____

_____

Overall, how would you rate your personal sportsmanship?

<———————————————————————>

Unsportsmanlike   Sportsmanlike

If applicable, how would you rate your team's sportsmanship?

_____

_____

_____

_____

Chapter 19: Shifting into the Team Captain Role

Advanced Quality #2 covers three approaches to leadership. Using the three spaces below, list them.

C_____ C_____ C_____

Circle the approach that is most like you. Explain why.

_____
_____
_____

Advanced Quality #3 is _____

Select two real-life "Sticky Situations" outlined under Advanced Quality #2 and describe what you would do to handle the situation. Be specific.

Situation #_____ Describe your approach to handling it.

_____
_____
_____

Situation #_____ Describe your approach to handling it.

_____
_____
_____

Which shift in language presented in Advanced Quality #6 on communication was most useful for you? Explain why.

_____
_____
_____
_____

Chapter 20: Cultivating a Captain-To-Coach Working Relationship

The Captain-To-Coach Questionnaire features "6 Pointed Questions" to discuss before the season starts. The sooner these six areas can be covered, the clearer your role will be during the season. Schedule a block of time with your coach to discuss the following questions. It is recommended that you bring this book along with a writing utensil to record the conversation. Do not rely on your memory for this exercise! Remember—agreements prevent disagreements. The time to discuss your operating procedure as a team captain should happen before the season starts and not in the middle of it.

#1. Specifically, what do you expect from me this season?

_____

_____

_____

_____

_____

#2. If you were to write a job description for me this season, what would it say? _____

_____

_____

_____

_____

_____

#3. How can I help you this season? _____

_____

_____

#4. What's the process to address problems and concerns this season? _____

_____

_____

_____

_____

_____

#5. What do I need to understand that I may not know now? _____

_____

_____

_____

_____

_____

#6. How will our personality styles mesh this year? (Refer to the chapters on T.E.A.M. Dynamics prior to covering this important question.) _____

_____

_____

_____

_____

Additional Information: _____

_____

_____

_____

_____

Chapter 21: Working with Officials

The content from this chapter does not apply to every sport, because some sports do not interact with officials. Even if your sport does not interact with officials, please complete this exercise.

In your opinion, why are first impressions important as you interact with officials?_____

_____

_____

_____

Describe a situation when you or a teammate didn't follow one of the suggestions in the chapter and indicate the result. Be specific._____

_____

_____

_____

_____

If you have ever had the opportunity to officiate a competition for younger athletes, describe what you learned about being an official. _____

_____

_____

_____

What was your biggest take away from the chapter on working with officials?_____

_____

_____

_____

_____

Chapter 22: Leaving A Legacy

Is your legacy as a high school leader important to you? Why or why not? Please be speci ic in your explanation.

_____

_____

_____

Was there a Legacy Leader high school athlete you looked up to as a younger person? Yes_____ No_____

If yes, why would you place them in the Legacy Leader category?_____

_____

_____

_____

Putting personal accomplishments and your win-loss record aside, what do you hope your legacy as a leader will be?_____

_____

_____

_____

_____

_____

_____

_____

_____

_____

_____

_____

Book Summary

Please check the content you completed/read.

___Team Leader Section: Chapters 1-18
___Team Captain Section: Chapters 19-22
___Certification Packet:
___Shared: *Parenting for a Season Of*
   Significance article and discussed with
   parent/guardian.
___Completed: the Parent/Athlete Covenant

After reading the book, I feel more confident being a team leader. Please circle your response.

Strongly Disagree   Disagree   Maybe   Agree   Strongly Agree

List the ideas from the book that were most beneficial to you and explain why. _____

_____

_____

_____

List the areas outside of sports where the content from the book will be valuable._____

_____

_____

_____

List three actions steps you plan to take as a result of reading *High School Sports Leader.* _____

_____

_____

_____

_____

_____

Workshop
Notes

*Coaching Team Leaders
and Captains to a
Season of Significance!*

Name

Craig Hillier Winning Edge Seminars www.craighillier.com

Opportunity is Nowhere

Seasons of Leadership

1. Awakening

2. Strengthening

3. Refining – *the better you get, the more difficult to improve.*

4. Empowering

Guage – Then Engage

Respond ability

Victor

Victim

S hame

You can __look__ back,
you can't __go back__.

B_lame_

N_ext_ !

Mistakes are F_reak_ O_ut_

great _moments_ D_eny_

Q_uit_

In a crisis, give yourself
__24 hours__ to respond.

"Either get bitter or get better."

–Jim Rohn

Significance =
meaningful
Important
Memorable

Play with Emotion

Don't be the

Emotional Player!

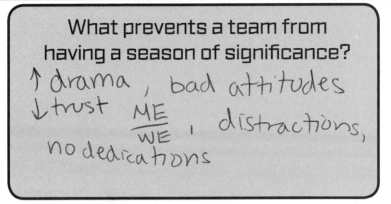

> ## What prevents a team from having a season of significance?
>
> ↑ drama , bad attitudes
> ↓ trust $\frac{ME}{WE}$, distractions,
> no dedications

Personal Evaluation

Three of my leadership strengths include:

1. _____

2. _____

3. _____

What holds me back from being a better leader?

_____

_____

Life theme or quote I live by: _____

_____

It would be beneficial for me to improve on what
area of leadership? _____

_____

Concerns I have about being a team leader include:

_____

I hope to be remembered as a team
leader who: _____

_____

_____

A Season of Significance

There are some ___team leaders___ who are not ___team captains___

There are some ___team captains___ who are not ___team leaders___

Setting the Stage

Show up ___every day___

Have ___integrity___

Remember all eyes ___on you___

Appreciate everyone's ___role___

Are ___up___ when others ___are down –___ my energy should be above the team

Keep winning ___in perspective___

Keep losing ___in perspective___

Avoid _____

Perspective Changes Everything

Resolving Issues

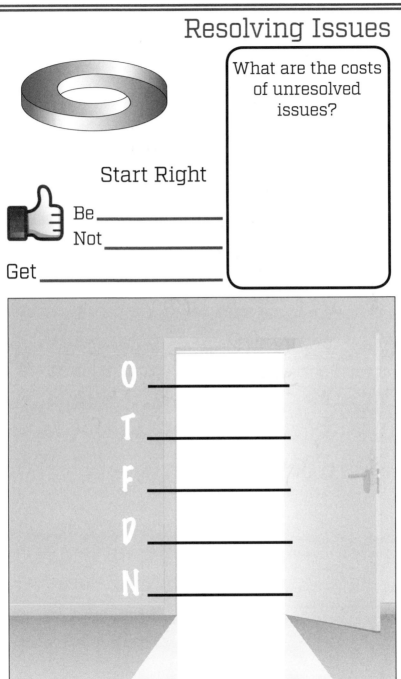

What are the costs
of unresolved
issues?

Start Right

Be _____

Not _____

Get _____

O _____

T _____

F _____

D _____

N _____

BONUS

Sportsmanship

Cool heads prevail

You can't control _a bad call_

The other team is the _opponent_ not the _enemy_

Arrogance is _ugly_

Win or lose, commit to _class_

Mistakes can _happen_

Be _respectful_

Watch _your mouth_

Know the _rules_

Know when to _speak up + shut up_

Volunteer to officiate a contest

Insight

Respond ability and
wait until calm to
address an issue

Action

Wait to talk to teacher
or a coach until emotionally
ready

Parenting for a Season of Significance

by Craig Hillier

Dear Parent of an Athlete:

Being a parent of a high school athlete is quite an experience. It can be thrilling one moment and heartbreaking the next. Some days you feel like an unappreciated taxi driver, while other times you feel like a hero when your son/daughter gives you a quick nod of the head and smile before the contest starts. Parents devote an incredible amount of time and resources so their kids can be involved in youth athletics. Almost everyone agrees that the life-long lessons gained from being involved in youth athletics can be a launching pad to a promising future. As a parent, you play an important role in establishing the value of participating in high school athletics.

Most likely your teenage athlete has removed this article from my book, **High School Sports Leader**—*Coaching Team Leaders and Captains to a Season of Significance*.

This article is really a report. It is based on the countless discussions I have had with athletes regarding the role of parents in athletics. **It's important to understand that the content you are about to read came from kids like yours and mine.** Athletes have encouraged me be their voice as I present my pre-season talks with parents and athletes. I take the role of being a reporter very seriously. I'm excited to outline what your teenager wants and needs from you, as they go through their high school athletic career.

My wife and I raised two kids who were both heavily involved in sports so as you read this, keep in mind that I'm a parent too. There have been several times when students' comments from my workshops became gentle reminders for me as well. **No parent is perfect.** We have all made mistakes despite having the best intentions. I say this because the content you are about to read is written in a tone of humility, not arrogance. My wife and I have battled the same issues other parents have when attempting to help our son and daughter navigate the inherent ups and downs high school sports provide.

Please read the following pages with the mentality that it is designed to **help us help our kids** create a strong foundation for life by experiencing the incredible value of being involved in sports.

The goal of this report is to get to the point and highlight parental practices that contribute to a season of significance. The chapter will also unveil parental practices that contaminate a season of significance. You will find the report provides solid, practical ideas and strategies that can be implemented immediately. Some of the content may serve as a gentle reminder as well.

Practice can be a physical action. For example, athletes go to practice to learn and improve their performance. Practice is also a mindset. For example, someone may adopt a personal practice to be on time for scheduled events. Parents, athletes, and coaches, rarely experience a perfect practice.

It seems it's more about progress than perfection.

Three steps to getting the most from this article:

1. Read the entire report and let the information marinate in your mind.

2. Sit down with your son or daughter and have an open, candid discussion on the content.

3. Create and commit to your own parent-to-athlete-covenant. (A report form is included at the end of the chapter along with discussion questions.)

We all want the best for our kids. By avoiding the contaminating parental practices and committing to the contributing parental practices, we can become a vital part of creating a season of significance for our children.

Sincerely,

Craig Hillier

"Prepare the child for the path and not the path for the child."
–Nathan Reeves

My personal experience as a coach, sports leadership workshop presenter, and parent of two high school athletes who have graduated, indicates most parents are great with supporting their son or daughter in sports. However, it's possible that even the sharpest parents have a few parental practices that can hamper a great high school athletic experience.

Let's examine the feedback high school athletes have shared with me regarding what can contaminate or conversely contribute to a season of significance.

Contaminating Practice #1:
Living out *our* sports career instead of letting the athlete live out their sports career.

How many times have you seen a parent live vicariously through their son's or daughter's athletic experience? If their kid performs well, they are all fired up. If their kid has a poor performance, the parent becomes distraught. It's as if the parent was participating instead of their child. As a parent, it's often difficult to wrap our minds around the fact that our playing days are finished. Personally, I still want to believe "I still have it." Sadly, that is not the case for me anymore. It became a reality when my son, who was 15 at the time, beat me for the first time in the 100-meter dash. When he started bench-pressing more than me, I really knew it was over!

My wife, Kelly, is a former gymnast. My daughter was a competitive dancer. Kelly could do the splits better than my daughter, up until her sophomore year. All we could do was smile and shake our head as we realized our kids were now beyond our current athletic ability.

We owe it to our kids to let them truly experience all that sports have to offer, from the mental highs of upsetting a state-ranked opponent to the lows of little or decreased playing time.

It's their experience—not ours.

Contributing Practice #1:
Enjoy the experience!

A question all parents must ask is, "Why do students participate in sports?"

All the research on the motivating factors to participate in sports indicates the number one reason an athlete is involved in a sport is to have fun! It's very common for young athletes to have dreams of being a professional athlete. In 8th grade, I believed the Philadelphia 76ers would be drafting me after an illustrious basketball college career. A long story short, not a single Division 1 college offered me a scholarship, and the 76ers didn't draft me.

With that being said, it's great for kids to have a vision to play at the next level. And as parents, we don't want to squash their dreams. However, it's helpful to know the odds of becoming a professional athlete.

The NCAA has compiled the research on the number of high school athletes who play at the college or professional level. Using basketball as an example, of the 158,000 male high school basketball players, only .03% make it to the pros. This amounts to 44 men being drafted. Of the 128,000 girls who participate in high school basketball, only 32 or .02% will be drafted for a professional career.

As you can see, the odds of becoming a professional athlete are pretty slim. So if that's the case, why participate if you can't advance to the next level? For fun! Sports are supposed to be fun. The thrill of working hard toward a goal, the camaraderie of being on a team with friends, and learning to take feedback from coaches in pursuit of improving, is fun! Now, is everything in sports fun? No, sometimes practice isn't fun. Losing is never fun. But how will they know if they are going to win or lose unless they participate? One thing is certain; when the fun evaporates from sports, participating becomes a struggle.

Contaminating Practice #2:
Critique your athlete's performance, whether they ask for it or not.

When I present to athletes and parents, I like to get the audience involved by incorporating a large group game of "Simon Says." Prior to the program, a handful of chairs are placed in front of the audience on a gym floor or auditorium stage. I also ask the meeting planner for a few names of loud parents who may not always be supporting with their words from the stands. The entire audience plays the game and a handful of parents have a "VIP seat" where everyone can see how well they play the simple game. Before the game starts, I ask the parents in the "VIP seats" to look back at the audience. It's comical to see the look of terror that appears on many of their faces when they look back at me. I once asked a woman, "What is going through your mind," after she looked back at 1,000 people in the gym. Her eyes got rather large and she said, "There are just a lot of people watching me," she added, **"There's a lot more pressure being up here than sitting back there."** I simply smiled and nodded in agreement.

As the game of "Simon Says" progresses, parents seated in the VIP chairs begin to make mistakes and sit down. I often will pause the game to make comments like, "I can't believe you fell for that." Sometimes I say, "Come on. . . what are you doing?" I also show a disapproving look or shake my head when a parent sits down after making a mistake.

One father made a mistake in the game and I followed up with, "Why did you put your hands down when Simon didn't ask you to put your hands down?" This comment caught him off guard. He said in an angry tone that was loud enough for everyone to hear, "I was trying as hard as I could. It's not easy being in front of all these people playing the game, ya know!"

I let his words resonate for several seconds, and I could sense the audience was becoming a little uncomfortable. Finally, I looked to the large group and said, **"The athletes in your school are doing the best they can too, so let's be aware of our words from the stands."** It was a risky statement on my part, and I wasn't sure if I went too far. Then thunderous applause broke out from the parents and athletes. The applause indicated it was the reminder message they needed to hear.

A game of "Simon Says" provides an incredible metaphor for athletes and parents about dealing with mistakes during a contest. No one was trying to lose the game. Everyone was trying to win. Sure, there were varying levels of commitment and experience, but everyone in the audience was competing to become the winner. And when people made a mistake, most of them sat down and thought, "I could have done better." In other words, they already knew they made a mistake. Given the opportunity to play again, they would try to improve their performance. The same philosophy is true when our kids make a mistake in sports. For example, a baseball or softball player doesn't walk up to the plate thinking, "I hope to hit into a double play or at least strike out." **Regardless of the sport, athletes are trying to do their best at all times.**

So you may be asking, "What am I supposed to do when my athlete has a poor athletic performance?" Here is what athletes said they want from parents after a loss or poor performance.

#1 Allow us time and space to recover.

Athletes do not want to hear an ESPN play-by-play breakdown of what they did wrong by a parent, as that is the coach's job. Most high school athletes simply want a soft spot to land after a loss or poor performance. Just like "Simon Says," they already know they didn't play or perform well, so they are not open to receiving feedback on how they messed up.

#2 Let us ask for feedback.

If your athlete has had enough time to digest the loss or poor performance, they may ask you for advice or feedback. When the athlete drives the conversation, you have the opportunity to share your thoughts. It's probably wise to pick one or two areas of improvement instead of rolling out a list of fifteen mistakes that need to be addressed before the next performance. You could also use a reflective question by asking, "As you look back, what do you think you could have done better?"

Many times simply saying, "It was fun watching you play," or "I loved watching you play," are the words they need to hear. These words are not judgmental, critical, or cynical. They indicate you understand they were performing the best they could and attaining a perfect performance is nearly impossible.

Contributing Practice #2:
Cheer for everyone on the team.

Wouldn't it be amazing if you, as a parent, were actively cheering during a competition and at the end of the game/contest a person you didn't know would ask, "Which one was your kid?" This question would certainly indicate you were supporting the *entire* team from the stars to the reserves. If you have ever sat in the stands and heard a parent cheer for only their son or daughter, you may have thought, "Do they understand there is an entire team out there?"

High school athletes often say in my workshops, "I wish parents would either encourage or be quiet." This is a powerful comment. It's very easy to criticize your teen, an individual who is either performing poorly, or the teammate who is considered to be less talented than everyone else. At times, this criticism happens during the competition, during a break in the action or during a conversation at home. It's tempting to find fault, especially during a poor performance. If an athlete hears his or her parents criticize other players, they often start to wonder if other parents are criticizing them. This can create unnecessary self-doubt within a team.

However, if parents adopt the "encourage or be quiet" approach athletes desire, a positive parental culture is created.

A young woman shared this story at a workshop. A junior is about to make her first start on a varsity basketball team. Her hard work had paid off. However, this meant a senior who had started in the past would now be the "6th person off the bench," a role she was not happy about. Coincidently, the mothers of the two players ended up sitting next to each other at the game. One bitter comment from the girl's mom, who lost her starting role, was returned from the mom of the new starter. Soon the two moms were shouting at each other. One parent shoved the other and suddenly it became a brawl in the stands. The police were called and both women spent the night in jail.

The two parents involved in this story missed the big picture approach. There is usually an ebb and flow to a starting line up. By mixing up the starting line up, it could actually help the team. If they had adopted the "cheer for everyone" mentality, this embarrassing story would have never taken place.

Student athletes have shared an important distinction regarding cheering and supporting that is valuable. Athletes say they think it's fine for a parent to be proud of them, but they don't want their parents to brag about them. Almost all social media platforms are filled with photos or videos of parents stating how proud they are that their son/daughter just won an award. Sometimes, a video is captured showing an individual accomplishment when it was a team accomplishment. The text with the video often says, "Look at *name*'s last game." Of course it's nice to keep family and friends in the loop on some accomplishments, but it can easily be overdone. Ideally, parents have a healthy balance of sharing/posting accomplishments without going "over the top" on how great their son or daughter is performing.

When parents consistently cheer and support everyone on the team, the positive attitude radiates to the players, coaches, and anyone attending a game or contest.

Contaminating Practice #3:
Unnecessary use of alcohol

As a football team is preparing to take the field for introductions. One player says to a senior player, "Hey, there's your dad." The athlete looks up to see his father stumbling to the stands and talking in a very loud voice. The player asks, "Is he drunk?" The young man is embarrassed, looks to the ground and simply says, "It wouldn't surprise me." His father's behavior became a mental distraction that led to the worst performance of his varsity career.

An athletic director shared this story during a workshop. Though this experience happened a long time ago, everyone in the audience could feel and see how his father's behavior still weighed heavy on his heart.

The story reminded me of the great movie *Hoosiers*. A parent named "Shooter" embarrasses himself and his son by showing up for a basketball game under the influence of alcohol. **Does contaminating practice #3 mean a parent can't legally consume alcohol? No. The keyword is unnecessary.** The terminology of contaminating practice #3 actually came from a group of students in Wisconsin. Consistently students say, "We hear not to drink or do drugs and yet before and after our games, parents are drinking, sometimes to excess."

If you have ever been around parents who are drinking alcohol before or after a contest, it usually starts off rather calm. After 90 minutes of drinking, voices tend to get louder, as do the opinions of what should be happening with the team, coach, or program. If drinking occurs before a game, the rough tone can easily carry over to the game. If it occurs after a game, alcohol can alter a person's thought process, and comments that would normally be private are said out loud. Inevitably, these comments tend to be reiterated to the coaching staff or the parent of a kid who didn't perform well. This can lead to unnecessary drama for parents, coaches, and the team.

When I was in high school in the 1980s, we would have social gatherings with parents and players after football games where there would be music, food, and fellowship. To this day, I can still remember how meaningful it was to have parents attend these events that were alcohol-free. The post-game events had a definite impact on me. My wife and I hosted several post-game player/parent events at our house that were alcohol-free.

For us, it was more important for the kids to see adults have a good time without alcohol than to bend to the wishes of a few parents who felt compelled to drink when socializing with other parents on the team.

Parental alcohol use is always a touchy subject. As parents, we need to be cognizant of where, when, and how much alcohol we consume. Based upon the students' responses, they are watching our choice.

Contributing Practice # 3:
Get involved

When parents of athletes are willing to get involved in a positive way, the season is always better. There are myriad ways to be more than a spectator. Most teams have fundraisers, social events, or even concession stands that need volunteers in order to be successful. It's possible there is a booster club that does an incredible amount of work behind the scenes to raise money to purchase equipment or hire additional coaches.

Unfortunately, it seems the majority of parents either sign up for the minimum amount "required" by a coach or don't volunteer at all.

The benefits of getting involved include:

- Getting to know other parents
- Getting to know other athletes
- Connecting positively with the coaching staff
- Adding resources to the team including equipment or additional staff
- Improving the program
- Showing support
- Gaining momentum for future athletes
- Having a lot of fun

Parents who are more involved have a stronger pulse on the program. Involvement can also create a stronger bond with your son or daughter's teammates and creates a stronger sense of community. **Bottom line, we are better when we are together.** Challenge yourself to find an area of contribution. No doubt, you will be glad you did.

Contaminating Practice # 4:
Stepping in too soon

The byline for this chapter is, "Prepare the child for the path and not the path for the child." The first time I heard this I remember nodding my head in agreement. Then I started recalling times when my kids faced a difficult situation. Instead of listening and asking them questions to help them "pull the answer from within," I either told them what to do or stepped in to soften or solve the problem for them. Most parents do not want their kids to have to deal with difficult or uncomfortable situations. Yet, they are very capable of handling and owning the situation.

Maybe you are familiar with the philosophy mother birds have when their baby birds are about to hatch. Mother birds will not pick at the shell. They will patiently wait for the baby bird to crack through the shell itself. Apparently, this process helps the bird become stronger.

If the baby bird has too much help cracking the shell, they won't be strong enough to fly. In other words, the difficulty they face coming to life prepares them for the rest of their life.

As parents, we can probably all agree, this approach is easier said than done. However, do we want our kids to lean on us every time something doesn't go right? **By empowering our students to figure it out and develop the courage and skills to work through a difficult situation, we are preparing them for real life.**

When my son was in middle school he and a few friends pulled a prank on a neighbor that went too far. The neighbor figured out who was involved in the prank as the kids were talking about it on the school bus. When the phone rang and I started talking with the neighbor, my son's face went white. Luckily, I didn't take the, "My son wouldn't have done something like that!"

approach. It was hard to believe he would participate in such a prank as most of the time he was a respectful, responsible kid. **But let's face it; all kids are capable of making bad decisions.** I promised my neighbor I'd talk with my son about being involved in the prank. Sure enough, he was a part of it.

Regardless of how the other parents were going to handle the situation, my wife and I created a plan to make amends for his role in the prank. First, he needed to knock on my neighbor's door and acknowledge the situation and apologize for the prank. While I stood off in the distance, he was in charge of the conversation. To say he was nervous is a huge understatement. But he did it. Second, he needed to figure out a way to make things right with the neighbor. This required him to talk with his cohorts and decide how each kid was going to do their part to make amends.

It's interesting to see how parents respond when their child messes up. As parents, my wife and I didn't look very good. We were the parents of one of the kids who caused damage on someone's property. **Ultimately, we were willing to look bad temporarily so he would learn a valuable life lesson.**

The powerful thing is, that lesson stuck with him. We didn't smile about it then, but we do now as he tells the story to others. He always ends with the lessons he learned along the way.

There will be times when your son or daughter will be in a difficult, tense situation with a friend, teammate, or coach. It would be tempting to prepare the path by drafting the email or making the phone call to the person or group involved in the issue. However, when we let our kids "break through" the *shell* of the situation, they gain the skills necessary for navigating through real-life disputes. Eventually, they will fly from our "nest" and lead their own life. **Hopefully, it's a life where they are confident in their ability to figure it out because you prepared them for the flight path.**

Contributing Practice # 4:
Supporting the coach

Coaching in high school is an incredibly difficult task. The pressure to win has never been higher. The amount of time and energy it takes to be a coach is substantial. Despite a minimum salary, coaches put in countless hours to build their program. The average tenure of a coach is shrinking dramatically.

Most coaches got involved in coaching because they love the sport and want to help, inspire, and instruct their players to become their best. How parents view, interact, communicate, and support a coach can be a large piece of the puzzle to creating a season of significance.

There are several parental habits that can support a coach or coaching staff. Based upon the feedback from athletes, parents who adhere to the following habits demonstrate support for a coaching staff. Personally, I know committing to this list is a challenge. There have been times when I have fallen short of supporting the coach. Again, there are no perfect parents. If we can maximize the following habits, our kids will have a better experience in sports.

Habit #1: Let the coach—coach

Imagine someone coming to your place of work or home who starts sharing ideas on how you could improve. Because they live in a home and have a job, they feel knowledgeable enough give you feedback. In addition, they share their ideas and opinions with your co-workers and neighbors in an unsolicited manner. Despite having the best intentions, how would you feel about this person? Most would think, "What are you doing here and why do you feel compelled to share your wisdom in my home or place of employment?"

Are there times when parents take a similar approach with a coach? They share their "wisdom" with anyone who will listen. As parents, we need to remember a coach has been either hired or at times is a volunteer in a non-sanctioned sport/program by a high school league. It is our job to be supportive by honoring their role even if you disagree with some of the strategies employed. (There are exceptions to this that will be covered later in this article.)

When we let the coach—coach, we are also teaching our athletes about the future regarding employment. Whether they like or agree with a boss, it's their job to be productive at work. There will be times when they will be working at a job where they don't like or agree with a boss or supervisor. Certainly, one option is to leave the job. However, it's also possible the next job will include a boss, supervisor, or co-worker they don't like.

If athletes can learn how to interact and be coached from a variety of coaching styles, they are not only learning in the present, they are also preparing for a future career.

Habit #2: Build a professional working relationship

There is a delicate balance of being friendly and supportive of a coach and overdoing it. The friendly and supportive parents are willing to jump in and volunteer when an opportunity presents itself. Examples could include taking a shift to work a concession stand, planning a pre- or post-game meal, or getting involved in a booster program.

When parents stretch the boundaries of a relationship by planning elaborate events or purchasing items or services with the unspoken hope of increased playing time for their child, a poor message is being sent. I recall a coach telling me how one mother was doing an incredible job as the president of the booster club. Yet, when her daughter started seeing less playing time due to the improvement of an underclassman, she suddenly resigned in the middle of the season. This decision revealed her motivation was not to help and support the team, rather it was to increase her daughter's playing time.

Habit # 3: Understand you might not have all the information

Most coaches spend a considerable amount of time preparing their athletes for competition. Depending on the sport, it's common for coaches to watch game film on the upcoming opponent and then create a specific game plan based on their observations. This often involves introducing a new strategy that could involve having athletes take a new or different role.

It's easy to walk into a contest, see a different strategy being used and ask, "What in the world is going on here?"

Normally, there is a reason for making a change or adjustment, and it's important for parents to give the benefit of the doubt before becoming critical.

I experienced one particular strategy change in high school basketball that surprised many parents in the stands. We were playing a home game against the number three-ranked team in the state with an undefeated record. Due to two key injuries to our tallest players, it was not looking good. Our coaching staff decided to implement a "stall offense." Basically, we would pass the ball around and not shoot unless it was a certain basket. This would frustrate the other team and a low scoring game increased the odds for an upset. The score at halftime was 2-1. Many parents were going crazy, as they had never seen this approach before. While our team ended up losing with a score of 15-9, it was the narrowest victory of the season for the opposing team.

It would be easy to be critical of this approach unless you knew the strategy behind it. In addition, the coach is not going to share the game plan with the parents, as that is his/her job.

Parents can support the coach by believing there is a purpose behind the game plan, even if it may not be totally understood.

Habit # 4: **Avoid coaching from the stands**

Maybe you have heard a parent yell instructions to an athlete that are contradictory to what a coach is attempting to do. The athlete hears their coach say one thing and a parent say another. Now there is confusion, which usually leads to an athlete making a mistake or turning in a poor performance.

The last thing an athlete needs during a competition is confusion. In addition, there are a lot of people who simply don't understand the game or how the game may have changed over the years. It's also possible a parent has never played the game their son/daughter is playing and simply yells things they have heard other parents yell from previous contests.

By avoiding coaching from the stands, we demonstrate trust and support for the coach and their strategy.

My friend Bill has a son who plays on a high school basketball team. During the preseason parent/player meeting, the coach said, "All the parents will sit directly behind the bench." At first Bill didn't understand this philosophy. As the season progressed, he started to understand the benefits of having parents sit together. First, it showed a physical presence to the players, audience, and opponent, that the program was a "united force." Bill also found himself more connected to the other parents as they were asked to mix up their seating arrangements and not sit next to the same parent. Bill noticed that by sitting behind the team, the parents were cheering for the entire team. They also became more aware of their words.

Bill tells a humorous story where one parent was verbally critical of the official's call. A fun-loving parent who brought blow pop suckers for the players to have after the game said, "Hey,

I think you need a sucker." The other parents laughed, but the point was made. According to Bill, it became a fun reminder and symbol to watch your comments from the stands and not get sucked into being critical. He also said parents began asking for suckers when they were feeling tempted to either officiate or coach from the stands. Maybe all the parents on your kid's team need to throw a few dollars together for some suckers, gum, or gummy bears that will serve as a reminder to "chew on their words."

Habit # 5: Understand the commitment required from athletes

An athlete's schedule can certainly take away from family time, social events, and vacations. There are times when a major family event is more important than a team practice or even a game played.

It's important for families to understand the commitment a coach wants and needs from his or her teenage athletes. Unless a major event takes place, athletes who are a part of a high school team, should attend every practice and game. Most sporting programs post a practice and game schedule well before the season begins. A game schedule is normally available at least six months prior to the season.

From a coach's point of view, it is very difficult to have a player miss practice or a game due to a family vacation during the season. If parents decide to go on a family vacation during the season there are two things to keep in mind:

Communicate the vacation dates with the coach as soon as possible. Springing the news on a coach that a player will not be available for a week because of a family vacation would be considered ill mannered. Most likely the coach will not be happy about the decision, and their reaction will be magnified if it is delivered very close to the vacation dates.

Understand there will be consequences for missing practice or competition. Most coaches discuss the difference between an "excused absence" and an "unexcused absence" in their pre-season meetings. Almost all coaches outline the consequences of unexcused absences from practice or competition. Some consequences could include sitting out a part of a game, diminished playing time, and/or extra conditioning upon returning to the team. While parents might disagree with the consequences, they have to understand a coach is counting on everyone being available for the entire season.

Part of supporting a coach is clarifying what is considered an excused and unexcused absence. Keep in mind, what a coach views as an excused absence in their program may not be seen as the same by a coach in a different sport.

Club teams and school teams. Sports have changed a lot in the past 30 years. There was a time when a sport was only played "in season." Today, there are many opportunities to play a sport year round through various club teams. This is both positive and negative. The upside is an athlete can really develop his or her skills by putting more time into the sport. The downside is athletes increase the odds of injury and becoming burned out by competing throughout the year.

A common conflict occurs when an athlete is a part of a high school team and also plays on a year-round club team. Most parents I talk with on this subject agree that an in season high school sport takes precedent over a club sport.

Exceptions to the contributing parental practice of supporting the coach. There may be situations where it's no longer possible to support a coach. These situations do not include the amount of playing time an athlete is getting or a coaching strategy. These decisions are a part of their job and most coaches will not even entertain a conversation regarding either of these issues.

However, if there is an unhealthy or toxic action that is taking place, it may be time for a difficult conversation. If whatever action is taking place is affecting the mental health of the players, you might request a meeting for clarification. Prior to the meeting it may be wise to read chapter 16 on *Dealing with Conflict*. The chapter covers approaching a conflict with an open mind as you may only have one side of the story. Depending on the situation, you will also have to determine who is going to be involved in the meeting. Unfortunately, we have all read stories about situations where an action or behavior from a coach is out of bounds and it needs to be addressed with the appropriate people. While these examples are very rare in occurrence, sometimes parents need to take the lead and examine an issue.

Keeping everything in perspective. It is unlikely you will agree with a coach's decisions 100% of the time. It's human nature to second-guess a situation after we have had time to process it. When a coaching decision wasn't favorable, it's easy to be critical. **Just like parents are not perfect, coaches are not perfect.** A supportive attitude for coaches will go a long way toward creating an experience that will set our kids up for a great life.

Contaminating Practice # 5:
Believe performance = worth

A father raced into the parking lot of the tennis court. He was talking on his cell phone about a business transaction. He continued the loud conversation near the fence until his wife, who was in attendance from the beginning of the match, tugged at his sleeve and told him to end the call. Both hands were now gripping the fence as the father began "coaching" his daughter with statements like, "Come on, go to your backhand," "This kid is not that tough." It's clear his actions threw his daughter off balance.

After watching for a half hour and anticipating his daughter losing another tennis match, he gave the fence one last push and said, "I can't watch this *#^% anymore," and stormed off while he dialed a client on his cell phone.

His daughter heard the tires squeal, as the father drove by the tennis court. With her father's absence, the young woman made a miraculous comeback to win the match. Unfortunately, the father in the story based his daughter's value on her performance. Ideally, parents consistently support their kids whether their performance is awful or awesome. They will be our kids a lot longer than they will be athletes.

Contributing Practice # 5: Create and commit to a Parent/Athlete Covenant

Harvey McKay says, "Agreements prevent disagreements." When expectations are clearly communicated, and each person understands their role and how to execute their responsibilities, a group will thrive. Expectations that are unclear and poorly explained can lead to confusion, frustration, and disaster.

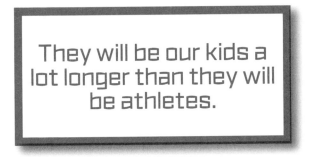

They will be our kids a lot longer than they will be athletes.

The final contributing practice involves creating and committing to a Parent/Athlete Covenant. A covenant is a mutually agreed upon promise between two or more parties. While some covenants are spoken, the covenant you and your athlete are going to be encouraged to create is written. A written covenant prevents future misunderstandings. It also provides a code of conduct reminder regarding how everyone involved will operate through the athletic season. Ideally, the covenant is placed in an area where everyone can see it.

Because each family dynamic is unique, it would be impossible and impractical to create a generic covenant that all families would feel comfortable supporting. **A covenant will only be effective when it is custom fit for parents and athletes.** Because our kids are all different in nature, a covenant should be created for each student athlete. Parents understand, what works with one child may not work with another child, as their needs, motivation, and goals are different.

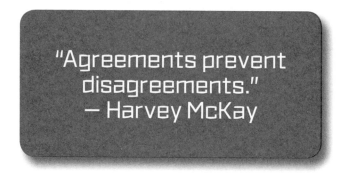

"Agreements prevent disagreements."
— Harvey McKay

Please have your athlete read this report before discussing the following questions. The best parent/teen conversations occur when both parties are focused and willing to open up with each other even though some of the conversation may be slightly uncomfortable. **However, the goal is to understand each other and create a covenant that eventually leads to a season of significance.**

Discussion Form: *Questions from parent to athlete*

What is your motivating force to be involved in your sport?

What do you think has been the biggest accomplishment of your sports career so far?

What life lessons has your sport taught you?

What has been difficult for you in your athletic career so far?

The report outlines five contributing parental practices. The fifth contributing practice, create a covenant, will be completed after discussing the questions below. Of the four practices listed below, which do you think I/we as parents are doing well? Please share examples if possible.

1. Enjoy the experience
2. Cheer for everyone on the team
3. Get involved
4. Support the coach

In your opinion, which of the four practices above could I/we improve upon? Please share examples if possible.

According to the article, the following parental practice could contaminate a season.

1. Living out our sports career instead of letting you live out your sports career
2. Critiquing your performance even if you don't ask for our critique
3. Unnecessary use of alcohol
4. Stepping in too soon
5. Basing your value on your performance

In your opinion, have there been times when I/we have mistakenly done one or more actions on the list? What were you thinking when you saw me/us take these actions?

If you were asked to give advice to parents of athletes, what would you say?

Discussion Form: *Questions from athlete to parent*

What is the benefit of having me participate in sports from your point of view?

What is fun about being a parent of an athlete?

What is the downside of being a parent of an athlete?

If a parent was involved in high school sports, "What life lessons did you take from participating in sports?"

If a parent wasn't involved in high school sports, "What life lessons did you take away from high school?"

The report discussed creating a written code of conduct, or covenant, that is customized to fit the needs of each family. Parents and athletes are encouraged to create and commit to a covenant. This covenant will outline the promises each party will make in pursuit of a season of significance. If a parent or athlete makes a mistake and doesn't honor the covenant, the hope is to learn from it and move on. No parent or athlete is perfect. It's more about progress than perfection. The goal of the covenant is to be clear on the attitudes and actions that will contribute to a great sports season. Take the time needed to state the promises you will make to each other. Once the parents and athletes are comfortable with the promises, write them out on the Parent/Athlete Covenant Form. **Feel free to create a second copy of the form for either a parent or athlete to display.** Ideally, one completed covenant will be displayed in an area where the entire family can see it as a positive reminder throughout a sports season.

Take the time and effort to complete the covenant.

Parent/Athlete Covenant

Parent/Guardian Section

I promise to adhere to the following practices to support a season of significance. If I fall short on one of the promises, I will re-evaluate and commit to improving.

Athlete Section

As an athlete, I promise to adhere to the following practices in pursuit of a season of significance. If I fall short on one of the promises, I will re-evaluate and commit to improving.

Student and Adult(s) Signatures   **Date**

A final message to parents of athletes

Both of my kids were a part of sports from the time they could walk. It's difficult to put into words how much fun my wife and I had being parents of athletes. We miss it!

We miss:

- Meeting their eyes before the start of game, seeing a quick smile and acknowledging nod

- Sitting on the edge of our seats during a close game

- The camaraderie with parents of their teammates

- Being a part of the booster club

- Seeing their friends at our house

- Traveling to tournaments

- Watching them mature into young men and women

The time will fly! Before you know it, they will be walking across the stage accepting their high school diploma. I sincerely hope you enjoy the journey as the parent of an athlete. By avoiding the contaminating practices and committing to the contributing practices outlined in this article, you will become a strong inspiration to your kids, as they pursue not just a season of significance, but also a *life* of significance.